FOR WHEN EVERYTHING IS BURNING

Dr. Scott Eilers, PsyD, LP

CONTENTS

Title Page	
Part I: Introduction	1
A Burial	2
The Pool	10
An Excavation	12
The Pool Part 2	17
Questions	19
Longing	30
Patterns	32
Longing Part 2	42
Problems	43
Vapor	46
Promises	48
Vapor Part 2	54
Part II: The Lies	56
The Six Lies The World Tells You	57
The Tree	61
Lie #1: Everything Is Your Fault	62
The Tree Part 2	70
Lie #2: You Can't Change Anything	72
3 AM	78

Lie #3: Something Is Missing	80
3 AM Part 2	87
Lie #4: What Feels True Is True	88
Hopeless	95
Lie #5: You're Not Trying Hard Enough	96
Hopeless Part 2	101
Lie #6: You Aren't Ready	102
Empty	109
Part III: Chainsaws	110
Carve A New Path	111
Empty Part 2	115
Silence, Critic	116
Rewrite The Research	120
Still Alive	124
Don't Let Them In	126
See What Nobody Else Can See	130
Still Alive Part 2	134
Hack The Equation	136
Look Beyond Your Limits	142
Two People	145
Ask The Right Questions	146
When The Past Bleeds Through	150
Two People Part 2	155
Nobody Knows You	157
Special Moments	160
People Like Me	165
Gratitude Takes Practice	166
Does It Make Me Faster?	170

People Like Me Part 2	175
It's All About Love	176
Pain And Purpose	180
The Bat Cave	183
I Love Discomfort	185
Release It	189
The Bat Cave Part 2	193
Neurological Superbeing	194
Shut It Down	198
Dark	203
Fuel	204
Recharge	209
Dark Part 2	212
Shame Executioner	213
Part IV: The Beginning	216
Remember Me	217
The Beginning	225
Haunted	228
Soundtrack	230
Thank You!!	231

A BURIAL

We are at war.

I think you can feel it.

It begins before you open your eyes each morning. Stress. Expectations. Adversity. Judgment. A seemingly impossible wall of tasks. An awareness that no matter what you accomplish today, it somehow won't feel like enough. A feeling of being tremendously behind in some intangible race. A resignation, a desire to simply survive until tomorrow, and an acceptance that you will never thrive. A sense of discontentment buried so far down you barely feel it anymore. A constant sensation of slipping further and further away from yourself with no end in sight. The weight and the emptiness of knowing how much of this you face alone. It doesn't relent until, finally, you fall asleep. Sometimes it bleeds over into your dreams, refusing to spare even your subconscious.

I feel it too.

The enemies in this war wear disguises. You aren't battling the entire world, although I know it can feel that way at times. You aren't battling other people either, not even the ones who have hurt you. The enemies aren't your school bullies. They're not your callous bosses. They're not your abusive exes. They're not your detached parents. They're not your disinterested or disbelieving teachers, doctors, or therapists. These people can all have devastating effects on your life, but they ultimately have limited access to you. The pain that never stops comes from a source you can't escape.

The enemies are the fragments of themselves that these people leave behind in your mind.

When people hurt you, they leave you with tiny traces of themselves. Reminders, remnants of the pain they created. Lessons they had no business teaching you. Unsolicited and unwanted changes to your existence. It doesn't matter if the hurt was accidental or intentional, physical or psychological. Like the pieces of a shattered vessel in a great ocean, they accumulate and disrupt the natural flow of thoughts and feelings that once existed within you.

These fragments aren't physical. They won't show up on any brain scan, no matter how sophisticated. The world's most gifted neurosurgeon cannot extract them. There is no pill, no injection, no supplement that can dissolve them. The damage they cause lasts far beyond the moment when the one who hurt you exits your life. Not even their death will "fix" you. A part of them lives on, inside of you.

Over time, we accumulate so many of these fragments that they change us into somebody else. We start to lose some of our gifts. Our passion, our desire, and our empathy begin to fade. And if you don't see the tragedy in this, that lack of compassion for yourself is a fragment left behind by somebody else. You shouldn't be OK with this. You are being stolen from yourself. Your joy, your vibrancy, and your excitement are being hollowed out from inside of you because you were forced to exist in a flawed and broken world. And you never asked for any of it.

Everyone's story is different, no two battle scars exactly alike. We all have our distinct versions of the who, the what, and the why, but the patterns created by the wounds are universal. You begin to see yourself as damaged, broken, and crazy. You stop prioritizing yourself. You find it harder and harder to feel love towards yourself. You judge yourself, criticize yourself, and shame yourself. You pull away from the world and start to hide parts of yourself. The person you once were, before all of this started, begins to fade out.

You entered this existence with an irrepressible love for yourself. You gave voice to your feelings from the second you were born because you held an unshakeable conviction that your needs mattered. You'd cry for hours on end if you felt like you had to, no doubt in your developing mind that if you were loud enough and persistent enough you would be heard and attended to. You trusted the world to respond appropriately to you, to give you the nurturing and care that should have been your birthright upon the beginning of your existence.

At some point, you began to lose that trust. For some of us, it's gone in an instant, so quickly we can't remember having ever felt it. For others, it vanishes slowly. Chipped away by every experience of feeling invisible. Eroded by every door that life has slammed shut in your face. Every experience of being disappointed, wounded, shamed, blamed, or invalidated drags you further from feeling like you belong here. Each day becomes a war of attrition, a journey through narrow and twisting corridors of relentless hostility and misunderstanding.

Can you remember your last moment of genuine joy? Unbridled excitement? Lasting pride? Unquestioned belonging? How long ago was it? Did the feeling last, or did it slip away almost as quickly as you noticed it? Did you genuinely *feel* it, or was it more of a thought, a mental acknowledgment that you'd experienced a moment that should have produced that feeling? I'm betting it was a faint little trace, like a memory of an early childhood vacation. You settle for reminders of having once experienced these feelings, staring at the hole inside of you where they used to be.

You have plenty of victories too. Achievements in your education and your career. Words of praise and affirmation from others. The majority of your life might even be positive experiences, but something blocks them from getting all the way in. You feel them knocking, know you should let them in, but something doesn't let you answer. Eventually, they stop knocking, and you're left with nothing to show for your wins.

Your natural state of loving yourself, caring about yourself, and valuing yourself, has been disrupted. Disrupted by the fragments of the people who hurt you. The feelings of love for yourself and trust in the world that you were born with become harder and harder to hold onto, like trying to keep water in your hands.

At some point, you become the voice. The judgment, intolerance, and misunderstanding that once came from outside of you start to echo within. When this happens you retreat further inward, searching desperately for a sanctuary from the pain. The trees wither and die, and the soil dries and cracks. You can no longer find safety, not even within yourself. Your last refuge becomes tainted and twisted by the brokenness outside of you. You repeat the messages you've heard, replay the patterns other people programmed into you.

"I don't matter."

"Other people are more important than me."

"I don't deserve good things."

"Nobody owes me anything."

"I'm broken."

"I'm unlovable."

"Nothing I do will ever be enough."

"Taking care of myself is a waste of time."

"I'm too fat/too ugly/too stupid."

"I don't belong in this world."

"I should just disappear."

The more invisible you feel to others, the harder it becomes to see yourself. You internalize their neglect of you. Every perception of failure, every abandoned dream serves to further suppress the inherent self-love you were born with. The world wears you down, like a relentless river carving a canyon through rock. You acknowledge it and accept it, wanting less and less out of life to soften your disappointment. Every time you're blamed for your distress, shamed for your feelings, told you aren't reacting correctly, that door slams shut harder and harder. The world is sending you a clear, unmistakable message:

Bury yourself.

Bury yourself as far down as you can manage to dig. Do it to protect yourself from everyone else. Do it so that you stop inconveniencing others. Do it because you shouldn't be this way. Do it because you're too much. Do it because the world is right and you're wrong. Do it because you're an anomaly, a statistical outlier.

Do whatever it takes to keep it buried. Spend money you don't have to keep from thinking about it. Distract yourself from your feelings with shiny objects. Have a few drinks to take the edge off. Eat too much, or starve yourself, or both. Just don't ever show those parts of yourself to the world again. Keep them far below, or they'll be picked and pulled at by the scavengers until there's nothing left of them to bury.

So here you are. You listened to what you were told, took in the feedback. You did what they asked; hid the parts of yourself that they criticized and exaggerated the traits that they praised. You don't celebrate your victories anymore, because that's arrogant. You don't voice your wants or needs anymore, because that's rude. You don't take care of yourself anymore, because that's selfish. You've followed the path that was worn for you, listened to the wisdom of your teachers and caretakers. Now I have an important question I need to ask you.

Are you happy?

Can people who live this way even feel happy? Or is it just

emotional anesthesia? I don't think they're the same thing.

You know what a hole in the ground is, right? A hole into which you place something that once had vibrant life.

It's a grave.

If you're living this way, constantly monitoring and modifying yourself for the benefit of other people, you are actively dying. Buried alive and dying a slow, suffocating death. Gradually slipping away from the world in the form you were meant to experience it in.

I did it too. I dug down as far as I could, I tossed everything that the world didn't seem to like about me into that hole, and I covered it up. I tried everything and took anything that made me feel or act like anyone other than myself. I tried so very hard to be the person the world told me to be. I offered everything I had to any deity I could think of in exchange for one simple request; make me something else. Make me acceptable to the world.

Slowly, I began to learn the art of appearing normal and happy. I practiced looking like I had everything I'd been told I was missing. I hid away the things that made me different. I stopped arguing and asking questions all the time and started agreeing with people more often, even when I didn't mean it. I found ways to take the edge off, ones that made me feel even worse during my private moments. I threw my shovel down and walked away, ready to finally be accepted, to be truly happy.

I didn't find happiness. I found an escape from most of the pain, but what replaced it was worse. It was nothing. An absolute emptiness I didn't know existed. I wasn't there anymore. I couldn't find myself, couldn't feel a thing. It was cognitive and emotional nonexistence, a life more terrifying than any of the intrusive death scenarios my mind liked to randomly insert into ordinary experiences.

I panicked. I decided to try and undo it all, to unlearn every strategy I used to artificially suppress myself. I worried that it was too late, that I was gone forever and there was no getting me back. It took years, and the progress was imperceptible from one day to the next. I thought about giving up so many times, but to my complete amazement, I eventually started to feel myself come back. Brief little moments here and there that proved the person I remembered being still existed.

It wasn't exactly like before. I wasn't as afraid of the world anymore. I realized that I was so much more frightened of the void inside me than anything this existence could inflict. I started to believe that there could be space for me in this life, even if I had to create that space myself. I wasn't as scared of my feelings this time either. They were as intense and as overwhelming as ever, but this time I wanted them to be there. Accepting them and welcoming them made for a much different experience than resenting and rejecting them. I realized I would trade the numbness for my full range of feelings any day, even during the lowest of my lows.

If anything I've said to you so far has sparked something inside of you or struck a chord that isn't often struck, please listen when I say this:

Excavate yourself.

Dig down once again and find everything that you buried. Keep going until you find every piece. Pull them out, one by one, and gather them back up.

Take back everything you entered this existence with. Defy the world and its expectations for you. Refuse the invitation to modify yourself for the comfort of others. Live without unnecessary concession for something that never concedes to you.

Love yourself like you did when you were an infant. Let the tears come when you feel them hiding behind your eyes. Give a voice to your needs, your wants, and your disappointments once more. Grant yourself every ounce of understanding, empathy, compassion, patience, and context that you typically reserve for other people. Show up for yourself the way nobody else ever has.

Invite your heart to be part of your world again. Experience life as a whole person instead of thoughts connected to tissue. Burst forth from the seams once more, but this time intentionally and with purpose. Don't hide to protect yourself. You're mostly hiding from things that have already happened, hurts that have already transpired, wounds that mainly exist within you. This life has already tried its hardest to break you, but the closest it could get was to bury you.

I promise you're still here, hidden but preserved, like a dragonfly in amber. Pulling yourself back up through all of those layers of earth is going to hurt, but it's the only way out of the hole. We can resurrect those dead feelings and put them back inside of you. It's possible to feel alive again.

That's the direction I'm moving in, and I'd love to bring you with me. I still have my shovel.

THE POOL

The first time it happened, I was at the swimming pool.

Swimming, playing, splashing.

Then everything was just gone.

There were no feelings inside.

They disappeared in an instant, sucked into the vacuum of space and replaced with a growling black void.

I got out of the water and sat on the edge, head in my hands.

Someone asked me what was wrong.

I didn't know what to say.

How does a child explain that they've gone empty inside?

I didn't even want to keep breathing.

Not because it was hard, but because it felt pointless.

Why breathe when you can't feel?

Why eat?

Why sleep?

Why talk?

Why study?

Why move?

Why do anything but wait?

And so I sat, and I waited.

Wondering if my ability to feel would ever return.

Or if this was the end.

AN EXCAVATION

If what you just read connected with something inside you, it means you're a bit different. It means that no matter how many people surround you, there's a piece of you that somehow remains alone and untouched. The intangible, indescribable rift that seems to separate you from everybody else isn't your imagination. It's real.

People might try to convince you that you're not so different. They'll claim to understand what you think, how you feel, and what you've been through. Maybe you even try to convince yourself that the separation is all in your mind. But there *is* something different about you. There always has been, and it's still there today. Fighting against it won't do any good. It's as real as the hand you're holding this book with.

You are an anomaly. The sooner you accept this, the easier the rest of your journey will be. There has never been anyone else exactly like you in the 300,000-year history of humankind. There never will be anyone else like you. Not even if humanity survives another million years on this planet. Not even if we discover a million other worlds with a billion people inhabiting each one of them. You're that unique. You're the only one of your kind.

You have roughly one hundred billion neurons inside your skull right now. Do you know what the odds are of someone having the exact same neurological structure as you? Seriously, do you? Because I don't. I tried to calculate it while I was writing this paragraph, and the answer my calculator showed had symbols and letters in it in addition to numbers. Although I don't know exactly how to interpret that, I'm pretty sure it means I'm right.

You'll have companions on this journey. Partners, friends, family members, and colleagues. But the only one inside of you thinking what you think, feeling what you feel, and seeing what you see is you. The story of your life is ultimately a story of one person, and you're the only one who gets to read every chapter.

It's a hard thing to accept, especially if you learn it early. It hurts to realize just how alone we are. But trying to escape the hurt only makes it worse. If you blur the lines between yourself and other people to try and absolve the loneliness, you'll only end up more frustrated and hurt when you find your way back to the same truth time and time again; nobody else quite gets it. Nobody completely understands what it's like to be you. They never have. They never will. And it's not necessarily their fault. Some of them probably try very hard to "get it," but they simply can't.

If you don't accept this truth about yourself, that you're a unique and distinct being who will never fully make sense to anyone else, your entire life can turn into a search for things you'll never find here. Total acceptance. Complete understanding. Unconditional belonging. You can't find these things in other people, even if they so desperately want to give them to you. Nobody can ever know you well enough to meet these needs for you. Nobody except yourself.

You've had thoughts that nobody else has ever had. Your feelings are created by interactions of thousands of memories that are entirely unique to you. Even the people who shared experiences with you don't remember them the same way you do. They were there, but they didn't see exactly what you saw or think precisely what you thought. Other people can't know you the way you wish to be known. There isn't enough time in your life to tell someone else your entire story, especially as you continue to add new pages every day. There are no words for some of your experiences. Some of your feelings have no names. Some of your memories exist only in images.

How could another person fully accept and understand you if they don't truly know you? How can they ever show you the appreciation that you deserve when most of your victories are internal and invisible to them? It isn't possible. At best, they will know certain parts of you, and they will only see those parts of you through their own unique and subjective lenses. They understand what it's like to be themselves, and from that perspective they extrapolate what they think it must be like to be you. They simulate the experience of being you inside of the experience of being them.

That's the closest another person can ever get to understanding you. A subjective simulation.

For these reasons you are, always have been, and always will be the most important person in your life. Nobody else even comes close. You can give yourself what nobody else can. You're the built-in countermeasure to everything this world lacks, every shortcoming it has. You can show up for yourself when nobody else does. You can understand and validate what will never make sense to anyone else. You're the answer to the questions you can't find the words to ask, the key to the box you've never been able to open. You are your first and final companion on this journey. If you aren't good company it's not going to be a pleasant trip.

That's why burying yourself, shutting your feelings down, and withdrawing from the world is such a harmful thing to do. If you aren't a full participant in this life, you lose your greatest ally. Forget about being lonely; you're truly alone now. Life feels numb, hollow, and empty. It's an elevator straight down, 10,000 floors below to the bottomless void.

No matter how long you've been hiding, no matter how

many fragments live inside of you, this isn't over. You're still in there. You cannot be removed, only pushed down. No matter how far down you are and how beaten down you feel, you can come back. You should come back. It's the only way you'll ever feel fully alive again. You can offer a hand to everything you buried so far under the ground, pull it all back out again, and welcome it with open arms.

If you want to make the most of this existence, you're going to have to fight against the status quo. It's culturally normal to hate yourself and your life just a little bit. We joke about it, make memes about it. We commiserate about our jobs, our partners, our kids, and all the dreams we've abandoned on the road to normalcy. We numb our feelings with behaviors, substances, and a little bit of denial to keep them from completely overwhelming us. This is the path we're shown.

I'm disenchanted with that path. I've walked it, and I've found it unsatisfactory. I don't want to be good at escaping reality. I want to construct a reality that I don't constantly wish to escape from. And I want you to do it with me.

I want you to disrupt your unconscious, automatic processes and allow space for critical thinking, examination, and evaluation. I want you to slow down your instinctual reactions and buy extra time to think things through, pulling yourself out of your homeostatic fog. I want you to take your life off of autopilot mode and climb back into the driver's seat where you belong. It's been made quite clear in the past few years that autopilot technology just isn't there yet.

Asking questions was the most important thing I did to excavate myself. When I was younger, I asked a lot of questions. I had a distinct and probably frustrating unwillingness to accept anything I found unsatisfactory (which was most everything.) The world told me, in various ways and through multiple people, to stop asking these questions. People also told me I'd get over it eventually, that someday I'd grow up and stop being so bothered by so many things.

I'm all grown up now. Do I seem less bothered?

Now I ask more questions than ever, but I don't ask them of other people nearly as often as I used to. I've found that, at least for me, it's somewhat rare to get a satisfactory answer to a meaningful question from another person. I'm the only one who knows all of my subjective truths, the only one who has been there through everything. I'm the only person who can answer most of my questions, and you're the only person who can answer most of yours. Ask them over and over again, patiently but insistently, until you find your answers. Don't stop until you're satisfied.

THE POOL PART 2

It won't last forever.

Nothing does, good or bad.

It will come back again and again.

But it will always relent eventually.

I know it's terrifying when everything changes suddenly.

I'm so sorry it happened to you.

I'm sorry nobody noticed.

I'm sorry nobody knew how to help.

It's not fair to you.

You're built a little differently.

People won't always understand that.

Won't always know what to do with it.

But eventually you will understand it.

You'll know what to do when it happens.

It won't be as terrifying.

It won't happen as often.

It won't last as long.

You still won't like it.

But you'll learn to be OK again.

Maybe it's hard to believe right now.

But some day you'll be much more than OK.

I promise.

QUESTIONS

I don't know why those things happened to you. I can't tell you where the people who were supposed to protect you disappeared to during your darkest moments. I wish I knew why nobody notices how hard you continue to struggle even today. I'm sure those are the answers you want, and I'm sorry that I don't have them.

I want you to know that it isn't your fault if you haven't found answers to these questions yet. Sayings like "everything happens for a reason" and "anything that doesn't kill you makes you stronger" put unrealistic and unhelpful pressure on us to find meaning and growth in every hardship. It's easy to feel like you're a failure if nothing positive has come out of your suffering.

Not every experience has a beautiful silver lining waiting to be discovered if you look hard enough or meditate long enough. Sometimes the inner lining of our experiences is just as awful as the outer shell was. Sometimes no matter how deeply you stare into something, all you find is layer after layer of pain. If that's all you've seen so far, it's OK to take a break from seeking. It's also perfectly acceptable if you never want to look again.

The questions I'm going to be encouraging you to ask aren't meant to help you solve the mysteries of existence. I don't have any special knowledge about the master plan for humanity or the secrets of the cosmos. My specialty is helping people solve the mysteries of themselves, and that's what these questions can help you do.

I love to look underneath things, to discover the unseen parts lurking beneath what I'm shown. When I was little, one of my favorite things to do was explore the forest and lift up rocks. There was always an intense moment of anticipation, a slight adrenaline rush. What would I find? Spiders? Worms? Beetles? Ants? Some bizarre creature I hadn't encountered before? The dark, hidden recesses always seemed so much more vibrant and exciting than the outward presentations of things.

I want you to start lifting up your thoughts and habits and looking at what hides beneath them. Take the time to get to know and understand your inner processes. Put the beliefs and memories that form the foundation of your personal norms under a cognitive microscope. If you're anything like most people, you'll discover that your reasons for continuing some of your most persistent patterns don't hold up to any real scrutiny.

Sometimes you'll find fear and insecurity tracing back to a single experience of rejection or betrayal, one defining moment from your past that dictates your interactions and your engagement with everyone around you. Sometimes you'll find constant efforts to prove your worthiness or your value to a person who isn't even an important part of your life anymore. Sometimes you'll find nothing at all. Behaviors with no purpose. Thoughts with no logic. Patterns that don't serve you.

Once you see what's underneath, you get to make some choices about what to do with your findings. Do you want to continue living out your patterns? Do you feel like they're leading you somewhere you want to go? Or are you running in circles, trying to escape a past that's already behind you? You're the only one who gets to make these choices. I just tell you where to look.

Do I like this?

You should like most of your life. Not all of it. Not every second of it. But most of it. If you don't feel this way, we need to find out why. This simple question is your guide.

Ask it all day long. I know it seems obvious, but humor me a little. Try it and see what you find. Ask it about every little thing. Do you like what you eat for breakfast? Do you like most of the people you interact with? Do you like how your bedroom is organized? Do you like how your clothes fit you? Question everything. Challenge every assumption you make.

Feeling drawn to something isn't an indicator that you like it; all it means is that you find it familiar. Routine, predictability, and sameness are the driving factors behind decisions made by your subconscious mind, which is where your more instinctual, primal desires come from. Your intuition about people, places, or activities. Your first impressions and your gut feelings. These sensations are primarily subconscious reactions to experiences based on pattern recognition. When something in your current environment reminds you of something from your past, part of your mind feels attracted to it because it correlates with a memory.

Your subconscious mind isn't concerned about your emotional health, happiness, or sense of fulfillment with life. It's only concerned with ensuring your continued physical survival and safety. It keeps you moving in the direction of what you already know, even if what you already know is abuse, invalidation, narcissism, or gaslighting. Whatever you're used to feels like home, and there will always be a draw to that, even if home was hellish.

Safety feels uncomfortable if you're used to abuse. Praise feels uncomfortable if you're used to criticism. Acceptance feels uncomfortable if you're used to rejection. Familiarity has an inherent gravity to it. That's how your life mysteriously ends up feeling the same even when the people, the places, and the activities change. If you don't consciously ask this question of yourself regularly, you'll find your way back to the same internal feedback loops over and over again.

We can also lose our sense of what we legitimately like

and enjoy through absorbing the beliefs and opinions of those around us. How many articles of clothing do you have in your closet that you rarely, if ever, reach for? How many books do you own that you keep putting down after a few uninteresting chapters? Do you keep buying the same "healthy" foods over and over again and then proceed to avoid them until they go bad and have to be thrown out? What about those songs on your playlist that you always skip?

We try, consciously and subconsciously, to shape ourselves to whatever archetypes we align with or want to align with. We accumulate possessions, habits, and hobbies that seem like they fit with how we see ourselves. All of these things take up space, time, energy, and money and you probably don't even like some of them. If you find yourself consistently moving away from something that seems like it "should" be enjoyable to you, don't blame yourself. Accept that maybe it just isn't for you after all and that it doesn't need to be a part of your life.

When you move away from long-standing habits that don't serve you, or when you finally allow something enjoyable into your life that you've denied yourself for so long, you build trust within yourself. Like an attentive caregiver, you ask the right questions, genuinely listen to the answers, and take action accordingly. Over time, this consistency and nurturing helps you see yourself as someone who cares and someone who can help. It allows you to build a life that's uniquely suited to you, something that works for you. Something you might actually like.

Who taught me this?

You're probably familiar with the saying "consider the source." We're flooded with an overwhelming amount of contradictory beliefs and advice on nearly every topic. Wine and coffee might extend your life by years, or they might shorten your lifespan. Never let a baby cry it out because it traumatizes them, but never rock a baby to sleep at night or you'll create a habit and spoil them. The other day a random guy in a parking lot told me I was killing the planet by driving a truck but he had a brand-new gas lawnmower in the back of his Prius. Life is complicated, and things don't always make sense. Considering the source is the filter for separating the helpful and unhelpful, the useful and the useless.

You also need to consider the sources of lessons and norms imparted upon you in the earliest years of your life. You weren't able to do it then; your mind wasn't physically mature enough to ask questions like this one. That's why you should start working your way back through these lessons now.

Nearly everything you know how to do and every belief that you hold was taught to you by someone else. Someone who may or may not have been qualified to teach you about that particular topic, or someone who clearly benefitted from you believing whatever they told you. Sometimes the people who know the least are the most eager to share their perspectives with others. Sometimes our caregivers are more concerned with how what we believe impacts them than how it affects us.

What do you think happens to you if the person responsible for teaching you something doesn't really know to do it? Let's say you're trained to deal with your anger by stuffing it, hiding it, and ignoring it. When your rage eventually reaches an uncontrollable, boiling-over point because nobody taught you how to skillfully express and release it, will you realize that what you were taught was wrong? Most people won't, at least not without help. The most common reaction is to blame yourself. To assume that, somehow, you did it wrong, and you need to try harder next time.

We can live our whole lives repeating the same behavioral patterns from the same ineffective lessons. We might blame fate, karma, or luck when our goals and dreams never come to fruition if we never stop to question if we've simply been taught an incomplete or unhelpful lesson. It's so easy for a lack of proper training followed by a few missteps to convince us of our own incompetence or inadequacy. You can travel that road your whole life if you don't use this question to assess what you've been told.

Let the lives of your teachers serve as your guideposts. How are they doing in whatever areas of life they claim to be knowledgeable in? Does the person who taught you about relationships appear to have healthy relationships? Is the person who taught you how to manage money in a good place financially? I'm sure some are doing well, but I'm equally sure you'll find that some people had no business advising you. The world is full of hypocrisy and misinformation. Always consider the source. Always.

Is it real?

I know you constantly try and think two or three steps ahead. You try to anticipate rejection, failure, or disappointment and eliminate it before it happens. You want to have a contingency plan for every potential issue you may face. I understand why you feel like you need to do this. I also understand the toll it takes on you.

Living like this drains you in every possible way. Your time, your energy, and your concentration are all finite. Most of your resources are spent on coping with disasters that will never happen. The constant mental battles and nonstop planning leave you with almost nothing left. The endless theoretical stressors keep you constantly on the edge of what you can handle, even beyond it sometimes, and much of what gets you there isn't even real.

Sometimes you turn to extreme coping mechanisms to deal with this chronic sense of impending doom that only you can feel. Drugs and alcohol. Excessive shopping or gambling. Unhealthy relationships with food. These powerful tools create very real, tangible problems if you use them excessively. Coping with problems that aren't real ends up creating problems that *are* real. Which you then have to cope with. This cycle can trap you so easily, and it can seem like there's no way out.

This question is the way out. It's the stress version of an elimination diet. Remove everything but the bare essentials. Reset your algorithm and redistribute your resources. Focus as close to 100% of your efforts as possible on the present, real issues and stressors each day brings. For most of us, that will be plenty. Don't waste your endangered resources on the future when the present is giving you all you can handle.

Ask it again and again for every stressor, every source of anxiety. Is it real? Not "could it be real if X, Y, and Z happen?" Not "wouldn't it be awful if this was real?" Is this an issue that requires your energy and attention at this very moment? If not, do everything in your power to focus on what's happening right in front of you. Your mind will fight back. It will always resist you when you try to change a pattern. You just have to outlast it. Come back to the present again, and again, and again. Ask this question hundreds of times each day if you need to.

Slowly, eventually, your mind will begin to relent, and the constant need to try and predict the future will fade. You'll have more energy, more brainpower, and more time to deal with your actual life, the one that's here right now. The only one you can change. The only one that matters.

What do I want?

Your life has a current, a flow, just like the little creek behind the house I grew up in. I used to love throwing sticks and leaves into the water and watching them float downstream. That was their only choice. They had no power, no sentience. They could only move in the direction of the current.

You have power and sentience. You have 360 degrees of freedom, but if you don't use it, you'll float downstream like a dead stick. Carried away to some predetermined destination that may or may not be satisfying to you. A life decided for you by circumstance, by averages, and ultimately, by other people.

If you want to choose your own direction, spend some quality time with yourself. Not busy, distracted, a-few-seconds-here-and-there time. Real time. Ask questions. Be patient. Treat your inner monologue like you're on a first date with it, not like it's the 30th year of a bad marriage. Strip away the jadedness and the frustration and start over with yourself. Share your hopes and dreams, your goals and your visions, and listen with rapt attention. Create a new beginning for your relationship with you.

This life can so easily drift towards emptiness and pointlessness if you don't have conscious, tangible goals. And remember that every goal is a rough draft. I'm not saying you need to plot out your entire future in a romantic afternoon with yourself, but you should have a general sense of which direction you'd like to be moving in. It's almost impossible to get anywhere in life if you're just winging it every day.

If you don't have at least a broad concept of what you want from this existence, you can't evaluate whether you're on the right path or not. If I wanted to drive to California from my home in Iowa, I don't necessarily need to plot every turn, every stop, or the exact time I'll arrive, but I do need to know that California is west of me. I can't just drive in some random direction each day and expect to like where I end up.

Looking back on hopes or dreams you left behind can also help you find your course. What have you abandoned on the roadside of the path to your current location? Is there anything worth going back and retrieving? Did you drop anything because someone else encouraged you to? If so, are you happy with that decision, or do you want to reconsider it?

You make hundreds of choices a day, and they all count. Each of them adjusts your trajectory, if only slightly. Calibrate your choices to your desired course. Align your decisions with the direction you want to move in, and you'll eventually reach your destination. It doesn't matter how long it takes. All timelines are arbitrary. Your trajectory is all that matters.

Why am I doing this?

Yesterday I noticed myself eating a handful of animal crackers my daughter had abandoned in order to play with the dog. I wasn't hungry. I don't like animal crackers. I had no reason to even be in the kitchen.

Why was I doing it? I didn't have a reason. There was no benefit to my actions at that moment. I was acting on instinct, running on autopilot. I was being a survival-minded mammal and not a conscious, rational being. See food, eat food, move on.

You'll be shocked if you get in the habit of asking this question. Shocked by how much of what you do in a day is absolutely purposeless behavior. Why did you pick up your phone in the middle of working on something? Why did you look up your ex on social media? Why did you buy a 20th pair of shoes?

When you ask yourself this question, it's going to go one of three ways. Sometimes you'll have completely valid reasons for doing whatever you're doing. You'll be satisfying a present want or need, working on something you value or that relates to your goals, or spending time with loved ones, to name a few examples. When you find your reason for your action satisfactory, carry on. Nothing more to do here.

Sometimes you'll find a reason for doing what you're doing, but the reason won't make sense. Sometimes we eat because we're bored. Sometimes we clean because we're angry. We develop unhelpful and unnatural associations between needs or feelings and behaviors. This causes a pair of problems; the original need goes unmet, and new needs are often created by the unhelpful behavior. We tend to abuse resources that don't serve their intended purpose because they don't provide effective relief from whatever was bothering us. Eating doesn't satisfy boredom for very long, so you're likely to keep going back for more food as soon as the boredom returns. Eventually you realize you've eaten way too much food and you criticize yourself for it. Now you feel ashamed. Also, you're still bored.

Sometimes you'll find nothing at all under that rock. No reason for doing what you're doing other than mindless behaviors or habitual patterns. You're doing it because you're used to doing it, nothing more. So much of your time, your energy, and your money get spent on nothing. That's where it all goes. That's part of the reason you always feel tired, even after days that weren't overly busy. It may also be why you never seem to have more money in the bank, no matter how much your income increases. Too much of it goes towards nothing. If you don't have a good reason to be doing what you're doing, put it down and walk away. If it doesn't bring you closer to your destination, it isn't a good use of your limited resources.

Asking this question consistently keeps you accountable to yourself and helps you spend your resources on what matters most to you. It's a tool to help you eliminate purposeless behaviors, wasteful habits, and harmful patterns. Use it often, and enjoy the space the answers to this question free up in your day.

Am I who I think I am?

What you consider to be your identity shapes your decision-making process. It guides you down certain paths and walls you off from others. You use the template of what you believe to be "you" to inform how you allocate your time, who you associate with, and what your goals for the future are. An inaccurate self-concept can cut you off from finding purpose and lead you away from defining moments in your life. It almost stopped this book from happening.

For most of my life, I didn't consider myself a creative person. I'd joke about how rigid my mind was and my total lack of artistic ability in any domain. Once, after I expressed this in a therapy session with a client, she asked me, "Are you sure about that? You seem pretty creative in how you do therapy."

That was all it took. I don't know where the idea that I wasn't creative or artistic came from, but it had been there as long as I could remember and I had fully accepted it. I had never, not once, bothered to question it. One person asking me if I was sure about it changed my life, and it changed my writing dramatically.

This book began as a fairly typical self-help manuscript. It contained good information that probably would have been helpful to a fair number of people and was presented in a familiar, straightforward narrative. It was a decent book. Not bad, but nothing special. The night of that therapy session, I wrote the first version of "longing," which you'll read on the following page. That was the moment that changed this book. I wrote it, I read it, and I cried. Then I started over on the book. I wanted the whole thing to sound like that, to feel like that.

Question individual elements of your identity, especially those that have been there for as long as you can remember. Whatever it is that you think you aren't or that you believe you're lacking, how sure about it are you? Are you absolutely certain you haven't locked doors on yourself that could be opened again? Take a look, and if you find something you aren't sure about, test it out. Find out who and what you really are.

LONGING

I'm not entirely convinced that I'm real.

I feel like, at any moment, I could just stop existing.

Not die exactly, but fade into some sort of ether.

To go back to whatever void I came from.

I don't want to be human.

I want to be a ghost, a vampire, an alien, a monster.

Anything other than me.

Other than THIS.

Disconnected.

Unwanted.

Rusting away in a corner, unused and unloved.

Too advanced or totally obsolete.

I don't know which, but they feel the same.

I want desperately for there to be something distinct about me.

Something I can use to find my people, my place, my species.

Some kind of compass that can direct me to wherever I was supposed to have been all along.

There must be others like me.

I feel like my answer is out there somewhere.

If I could just meet that right person, find that right place, discover that right truth, everything would finally make sense.

I need something that binds me to this world.

Something that connects me to other people.

Because right now, there's nothing.

Just an empty hollow where the connection should be.

PATTERNS

Once you know where to look, you'll start to see patterns in everyone. Universal bad habits we all seem to pick up. Unwanted yet tragically inevitable side effects of existing in an imperfect world. I want you to start looking for them in yourself. They're like photos with hidden images; you won't see anything at first, but once you notice what you're supposed to be seeing, it jumps out at you every time. You can never unsee it.

These are the patterns we use to kill our feelings. They shape us, form us to be more acceptable to the world and less acceptable to ourselves. They're the dirt piled on top of your living grave. Look for them in your thoughts and in your words. See how many of these you find inside yourself.

Self-invalidation

This may sound like:

- "Other people have it worse."
- "It wasn't all that bad."
- "I shouldn't have expected anything different."
- "Suck it up and move on."

We learn to self-invalidate through being invalidated by others. Sometimes people find our feelings or our struggles inconvenient, so they propose the quickest "fix" available; they try and convince us not to have them anymore. They encourage us to ignore or hide our pain, our anger, and our sadness for their benefit. Eventually, we start doing it to ourselves. It stops being something we have the ability to do when we feel like we need to and becomes a natural reaction to distress. The external voice of invalidation becomes an internal voice, a voice that never quiets.

When you invalidate your emotional reactions to a situation, you're essentially trying to command your feelings to disappear. To skip the part where you have to feel them and move right to the part where you feel "normal" again. I know that some of these feelings seem enormous, like they could consume you entirely or pull you into an inescapable black hole if you let yourself experience them in their fullness. I completely understand why you're terrified, why you would do anything to avoid them.

The problem is that ignoring them doesn't work. Not all feelings fade with the passage of time. Little ones do. Minor stressors and inconveniences will heal on their own without intervention from you or anybody else. Get cut off in traffic, and you forget about it by tomorrow. Like a stubbed toe, it hurts most intensely right away, and the pain gradually fades into nothing.

However, there's a deeper set of feelings inside of you that don't fade with time. Grief. Trauma. Betrayal. Failure. Rejection. They make a home inside of you, and they don't leave just because time has passed since the event that created them. They lie in wait within you, trying to surface from time to time. When you invalidate them, all you're doing is pressing the snooze button. They'll try again soon.

The only way to get rid of these feelings is to release them from the prison inside of you. To let them ripple through your mind and, sometimes, through your body. You might need to cry, yell, or scream. You might need to shake or collapse. It might look and feel a little like an exorcism. That's okay. You might need to do it more than once. That's also okay.

Try to organically allow those deeper feelings to express themselves. Don't go searching for them or try to force them to surface, but don't keep them locked away forever either. Allow them to come when they want to come, and allow them to fade when they want to fade. Just please stop cramming your feelings about every painful experience you have into a finite container inside of you. Eventually, that container will explode.

Life deferment

This may sound like:

- "I'm not that important."
- "Everyone else comes first."
- "My life isn't really about me."

Living for more than just yourself is a beautiful thing. Living only for something beyond yourself is a terrible thing. Chronically placing yourself last on your own priority list makes you feel disconnected, isolated, and worthless. If you wait until everyone around you is doing fine before you allow yourself to focus on you, you will never focus on you. That day won't arrive.

You can't give your all to anything unless your emotional health is relatively stable. In a way you can, but "your all" won't actually be the best of you or the most you're capable of. It'll be a pale imitation of your genuine ability to love and help others because nobody is loving and helping you. That's your most important job, no matter who you are.

Purpose is important, but it can't be a substitute for self-care. Your calling, whatever it may be, cannot take the place of having a good relationship with yourself and taking care of yourself. Neglecting those responsibilities isn't sustainable, and it will eventually catch up with you. Focusing exclusively on serving other people when you aren't in a good place mentally is a socially acceptable way to avoid doing the more complicated and often more painful work of learning how to care for yourself.

We would never expect these things of another person. That they sacrifice themselves every day, treat themselves like an absolute nothing. By asking ourselves to do what we would never ask another to do, we mark ourselves as different. We isolate ourselves from humanity, and we exacerbate and exaggerate the inherent loneliness and isolation we already feel. Forcing ourselves to play by different rules than everybody else makes us feel like aliens on a hostile planet.

The only reason you feel inferior to others is that you're acutely aware of your every flaw, every failure, and every misstep. This makes you seem more damaged, more broken, and more worthless than other people because you don't have this level of access to them. That's the only reason it's so easy to put everybody on a pedestal and devalue yourself; you know too much about you. You aren't less important than anybody else. You only feel that way.

Before you focus on becoming a caretaker of others, become a caretaker of yourself. You aren't exempt from needing love and support, and you're the only person who can theoretically provide them for yourself 100% of the time. Use your foundation of self-care as a jumping-off point for taking care of everybody else or living out your mission. Otherwise, you'll just run yourself dry.

Making excuses for the broken world

This may sound like:

- "Nobody owes me anything."
- "Life's not fair."
- "Everyone is just doing their best."
- "It is what it is."

We're encouraged by many to accept things the way they are. To stop questioning, stop wanting, stop being angry and just go with the flow. Sometimes I hate the flow, and I'm pretty sure the flow hates me sometimes too.

I want you to ponder this question; are you sure the world

doesn't owe you anything? Why shouldn't it? Is there any legitimate reason we shouldn't be able to expect things like safety, respect, and validation from our environment? Do you believe that nobody deserves these things, or that just you specifically are unworthy of them? If it's only you, what's the justification for that? What separates you from the rest of humanity?

I understand that wishing the world was different doesn't change anything, but that doesn't mean you should stop wishing. The world won't always give you what you need, and it's certainly important to recognize that and live accordingly. But when we give the world a free pass, we invalidate our own unmet needs. If nobody owes you anything, then it's foolish of you to expect anything from anyone. I can't get on board with that. That's the logic that abusers and manipulators use to brainwash their victims into not leaving them. I'm not OK with abuse rhetoric becoming a culturally accepted paradigm.

Every visionary, every leader, and every hero has been driven primarily by frustration, hurt, and anger towards the world. Martin Luther King Jr. Jesus of Nazareth. Mahatma Gandhi. Nelson Mandela. Abraham Lincoln. Every one of them looked at the world the way it was during their respective times and asked, "Is this really our best?" Can you imagine if the dream speech or the emancipation proclamation began with "nobody owes you anything?"

If you lend money to a friend and it becomes clear that he's never going to pay you back, you may give up on trying to collect from him, but it doesn't mean he stops owing you. There's a difference between being owed something but accepting you won't ever receive it and not being owed something at all. Don't confuse the two.

You have lent the world something. Your existence. You're here, vulnerable and human. Your nervous system allows you to feel pain caused by others. Your limbic system allows you to feel rejection, alienation, and hatred. These aren't optional parts of existence. You can be abused, bullied, manipulated, and even killed, and you aren't allowed to opt out of these parts of life without dying. I know what it's like out there, and I absolutely believe you're owed something for what you're forced to face each day. Accepting unacceptable things isn't peace; it's denial.

Your feelings are valid. Your frustrations, your pain, your anger; they're real, they matter, and they have every reason and every right to exist. This world is a bit broken, more so for some people than others. If you aren't one of the fortunate few, existence itself can be painful. I'll acknowledge that for you, even if nobody else will. I'd like you to try and do the same.

Trying to disappear

This may sound like:

- "I don't need anything."
- "Everything is fine."
- "You don't need to worry about me."

Many of us learn to make ourselves small and quiet when we're young. Children are to be seen and not heard. Standing out brings you unwanted and sometimes unpleasant attention. We're taught how to blend in. Be a part of the crowd. Be a cog in a great machine. Don't rock the boat.

As we mature and our relationships become deeper and more complicated, these early childhood patterns morph into more sinister, more dangerous dynamics. Passive communication. Difficulty setting and holding boundaries. Excessive and unhealthy dependence or independence, or a bit of both at the same time. One-sided friendships or romances. You slip further and further into the "don't worry about me" zone. A zone where you essentially exist as little as possible. A zone that only exists to make other people more comfortable.

Being as small and invisible as possible is highly convenient for everyone around you, so be prepared for them to reinforce this behavior. They'll praise your strength and your independence. They'll marvel at how "well" you are handling everything, which they judge based on you not appearing to need any help from them. Most people assess your behaviors primarily from the perspective of how those behaviors impact them, not how they impact you.

You don't need to protect other people from yourself anymore. You never did, no matter what they said or how they acted. You're not a mistake. Your feelings are not a problem. Your existence is not a burden. Every time you use your words or your actions to try and shrink your footprint in this world, you diminish your worth in your own eyes.

It's OK if your wants, needs, feelings, or existence itself are inconvenient for others. They say don't rock the boat. I say it's your boat, and you can do whatever you please with it. Just don't hide in the hull of your own boat, listening to the sounds of everyone else enjoying your life while you shrink away.

<u>*Excessively placating yourself*</u>

This may sound like:

- "I need a drink."
- "I can't adult today."
- "Time for some retail therapy."

When you decide to quell your feelings instead of experiencing them and dealing with them, you teach yourself a damaging, dismissive lesson. Like the parent who distracts a child with cartoons and ice cream when they're anxious about a legitimate concern, you subtly communicate to yourself that your feelings are wrong, inappropriate, not worthy of being taken seriously. You try to stop the feeling from being felt instead of addressing the cause of the feeling.

This eventually makes you into a shell of a person. You

become your coping mechanisms. You identify with them. They become your hobbies, your passions. The things that feel the best are the things that help you not to feel. You create an internal feedback loop. Have feelings, ignore feelings by doing something else.

Gradually, you start to avoid life altogether. You become chronically numb, your affect constantly blunted. You feel less of the distress, but as a side-effect, you feel less of everything. Life takes on the sensation of observing it through a one-way mirror rather than experiencing it firsthand.

This pattern also infantilizes you. It teaches you that you don't have the skills to handle adversity and prevents you from developing them. You become fearful and avoidant, hoping to escape being noticed or having anything asked of you. Life becomes dark roads and closed signs as your comfort zone shrinks to next to nothing.

If you want your feelings and experiences back, you have to spend less time numbing. You have to stop living in fear of the pain and the distress and learn skills to cope with them instead of avoiding or ignoring them. All human emotions have a shared genesis within the mind, and there is no method for anesthetizing the unpleasant feelings while keeping the pleasant ones. All you can do is set the range. Set it low by constantly placating yourself, and your entire life becomes numb.

Spiritual bypassing

This may sound like:

- "Nothing really matters."
- "This life is just an illusion."
- "You are only an observer of your own life."

Nothing has the potential to shut down your unpleasant feelings, at least temporarily, quite as definitively as convincing yourself that none of it matters or that it's all artificial. These messages come in many forms, but the core concept is that all of the suffering and strife you experience in this life is somehow trivial, unimportant, or even imaginary. We're highly susceptible to messages like this during our darkest times. The concept of a philosophy or worldview that can take away all of your pain in an instant is incredibly attractive, particularly when you're in a place of vulnerability and desperation.

I promise you, I want this to be real just as badly as you do. But it isn't. You can't just put up a spiritual filter between yourself and your life, or the world in general, and say that none of it matters. It's anxious avoidance masquerading as faux-enlightenment; nothing more.

This life and your experiences in it, including the horrible ones, are genuine, and they matter tremendously. Abuse is real. Assault is real. Suffering is real. Genocide is real. Poverty is real. War is real. None of it should be, yet all of it is. We live in a broken, fallen world, and that truth is something we must all cope with each day. Trying to convince yourself that this life is just some kind of test or illusion is simply another way to avoid the worst of it. For better or for worse, you are here.

You can't meditate your way out of a traumatic past. You can't escape your pain by discovering an unblemished inner being living inside of you. There's no ancient wisdom that can eradicate all of your suffering. The only way out is through.

Self-sabotaging

This may sound like:

- "I shouldn't get my hopes up."
- "I wonder when the other shoe will drop."
- "Nothing good lasts."

When you expect to experience failure and disappointment, sometimes you try to strike first. You withdraw your name from consideration so nobody has the opportunity to reject you. You intentionally share off-putting information early in a relationship as a "test." You pull the rug out from under yourself before anyone else has a chance to. Somehow, hurting yourself feels preferable to being hurt by somebody else.

When you do this, you always end up "right." You anticipate pain, you experience (self-inflicted) pain, and you feel justified in your actions. If the pain was inevitable, why not get it out of the way as soon as possible? Why not at least be in control of when and how the pain comes?

Except I think you know the answer. I think you know that it still hurts, no matter how much anticipatory pain you experience. The pain you inflict upon yourself is just additional pain. Substitutions aren't accepted. You can't pre-suffer. There's no way to make a down-payment on death, or loss, or rejection.

Let's say you were training for a boxing match. Which of these two strategies seems like it would be more likely to lead to victory?

>   A. Practice a range of boxing-related skills, including jabs, hooks, feints, and footwork.
>   B. Pay your friend to punch you in the face repeatedly.

Self-sabotage is choosing option B. It's trying to toughen yourself up by experiencing constant emotional distress. It's the hope that, after enough damage is done, your limbic system becomes calloused to the unpredictable, chaotic nature of our world.

Sometimes your self-sabotage is the only reason you experience the pain. Sometimes the adversity you try to get in front of isn't as inevitable as it appears. Shift your efforts from constantly trying to hurt yourself before anyone else has the chance to learning how to handle and, sometimes, dodge the pain. I promise this way hurts a lot less.

LONGING PART 2

You know how sometimes.

In the middle of a parking lot.

The concrete is cracked just enough.

For a single blade of grass to poke through.

It's a miraculous feat, really.

That a living thing can grow in such a harsh environment.

There's no shade.

The soil is covered up.

Everything around it is barren and dry.

Yet, somehow, the grass survives.

I think that you are like that single blade of grass.

Standing boldly and brightly.

In a sea of hot concrete.

Lacking the nourishment that you need to thrive.

Nourishment which others have.

And take for granted.

You are just as real as the others.

You're just far away from them.

It won't be like this forever.

PROBLEMS

If you start asking more questions and practice disrupting the patterns that kill your feelings, changes will follow. Initially, these changes may feel like problems. Your emotions may intensify as your connection to your life grows. You'll be more in tune with your day, and that will be a mixed experience. There may be fear that accompanies these changes. Some of this fear will come from you, and some of it will come from other people.

People don't like change, and they often struggle to differentiate between positive changes and negative changes. All change inherently carries an element of threat because it provides a novel stimulus, something unfamiliar. Our minds naturally resist and fear change, and they feel particularly threatened when the change occurs in someone close to us. Be prepared for the most important people in your life to question the wisdom of what you're doing. Don't over-interpret their hesitancy, their concern. It doesn't mean that what you're doing is wrong or bad. It means that what you're doing is different.

Other people don't like it when they see someone doing something they've given up on. There's a certain level of resignation that is culturally normal. Dreams die. Goals go unrealized. Compromise and complacency happen. People accept these things by convincing themselves of their inevitability. They tell themselves that nobody follows their dreams, that everyone is some degree of unhappy, and it's just the way things are. They need to believe that everyone buries their feelings and lives a blunted, emotionally flat life to cope with the fact that they bury their feelings and live a blunted, emotionally flat life.

When you break out of your acceptance of these things, you aren't just disrupting your coping system; you're disrupting theirs too. They'll see what you're doing, and they might not like it. By refusing to continue to accept what they've accepted, you inadvertently challenge their worldview. They're forced to question whether they gave up on their dreams prematurely, whether their unsatisfactory life was really as inevitable as they tell themselves. They may become jealous, bitter, or resentful. Or they may just cut you off.

If you want to break out of the patterns that keep you stuck, you'll have to learn to be OK with the people around you being uncomfortable sometimes. Seeing your change may confuse them or alarm them. Seeing your progress, your brighter affect, and your increased resilience might bother them, even if they love you and care about you. You'll need to resist the natural pull of aligning with them, agreeing with them, and living like them. That pull is very real and very hard to resist. Our minds are built for social conformity. We unintentionally and unconsciously take on the perspectives, attitudes, and behaviors of the people closest to us. We're social creatures.

As the lid you've placed over your emotional intensity container begins to lift, you'll start to feel all of your feelings more intensely. The frustration, the anger, the sadness, and the hurt, but not just those. Everything becomes stronger. Joy. Excitement. Love. Connection. Contentment. Your days will feel more alive. The colors will look brighter. Music will have more depth. That "just going through the motions" sensation will start to fade. It will be wonderful and terrifying and joyful and overwhelming.

There will be ups and downs, good times and bad times. That's the unavoidable truth of living in an imperfect world. But you are so much more resilient, more capable, and more powerful than you realize. You've weathered so much already, and I know it took so much out of you. You might feel like you can't handle any more pain, but it's the numbness that prevents you from recovering. You can't recharge from everything you've been through if you aren't able to feel things like love, joy, or accomplishment.

Sometimes we feel like we need a fresh start to change course. A clean slate, absolution from the past. Let's give you one right now. Nothing special needs to happen to start over. You don't need to wait for a bolt of lightning to shoot down from the heavens and shock you into forgiving yourself. You hold the ability to grant yourself clemency every second of every day that you exist, and you don't use it.

Use it now.

Say you forgive yourself. Say that you'll no longer hold your present self responsible for choices made by your past self. Say that you'll do your best not to count what's already transpired against your future self. Say these things to yourself again and again because feelings fade but patterns stick. Do whatever it takes, but don't forget it. Every moment can be a new start if you'll allow it to be once.

It's OK to be afraid of what may come of this. Much of what I will be asking you to do isn't "normal." It's also OK if you don't know how to deal with difficult emotions yet. That's what the rest of these pages are for.

VAPOR

I pushed into my mattress with all of my strength.

Tried to condense my body into the springs.

I wanted to become vapor.

I dreamed that my body would turn ethereal.

It seemed like the most efficient way to end this.

If I could just lose my physical form.

So many of my problems would disappear.

Then I could just float around the world.

Observing without participating.

Immune to the pain of not having a home.

Spared the embarrassment of my isolation.

Unfazed by my lack of connection with others.

I fantasized about becoming fog.

A grey, dreary cloud of mist floating in the wind.

Attached to nothing.

Gliding above humanity.

A part of nature.

No thoughts, no feelings.

No memories, no wounds.

Just vapor.

PROMISES

I promise that you aren't alone

So many people believe they're beyond hope or irreparably broken. It isn't just you, even if it feels that way sometimes – maybe even most of the time. Others with similar struggles are hiding all around you in plain sight. Silent allies in an endless war. Like you, they put on a brave face so that nobody worries about them or judges them. You meet them every day. They scan your groceries. They deliver your food. They manage your finances. They teach your children. They clean your teeth. They fix your car. They're next to you on the treadmill.

You don't see it in them because, like you, they've been taught to bury it. They escape. They numb. They invalidate themselves. They do what they think they're supposed to do to get through the day and keep the darkness hidden. They look fine to you, their pain worn only on the inside. And that's precisely what they think when they meet you. "They're fine." You meet, you hide your respective scars, and you both go about your day believing you're all on your own.

There's still a tremendous stigma against people who don't automatically feel good most of the time. Sayings like "vulnerability is weakness" are slapped on t-shirts and bumper stickers to remind us of just how unacceptable our distress is to others. You cross paths with people every day who understand some of what you're going through, people who share elements of your journey, but you're so conditioned to never admit to your struggles that you miss most of these connections.

I know how it looks. You see everyone driving to work, getting their groceries, going on dates, picking their kids up from school, and you think, "wow, everyone except me has everything under control. What the hell is my problem?" But haven't you done most or all of those things while you're crying inside? Don't you think people have looked at you on your darker days and thought, "wow, they seem to be doing okay. What the hell is my problem?" I guarantee that they have. And I guarantee that you aren't alone in this.

Billions of people struggle with their mental health. That doesn't mean they feel exactly what you feel or struggle in the same way that you do, but it most definitely means that you aren't the only person in the world who isn't "okay." Not even close. The loneliness and isolation that you feel are partially fake. They're the outcome of the façade of society, the consequence of the exterior of functionality that we're all trained to present with.

I promise not to over-simplify

There's no "one simple trick" that can dramatically alter the way your brain functions. Your mind has more controls than the cockpit of a commercial airliner, more pathways than every road in the world combined, more circuity than every electronic device in your home. Millions of neurons activate in response to everything you experience, every second of every day.

Anybody who claims that most of your problems can be solved with a single intervention like positive thinking, meditation, diet, exercise, or affirmations either doesn't understand how the brain works at all, or they completely understand and they're intentionally misleading you for personal gain. Neither of these is a good reason to listen to them or give them your money. You're much too complex to be "fixed" by a single solution.

Like spiritual bypassing practices, these claims are incredibly attractive. I want them to be true as badly as anyone. If you could genuinely cure your depression by changing your diet or heal your trauma by being more mindful there wouldn't be millions of people trying desperately to find a good therapist or a tolerable medication. We wouldn't lose people to suicide every day if you could fix everything by practicing positive mantras or working out.

Honestly, these claims offend me. I see just how hard some people have to work to try and be happy. All the strategies they try, the books they read, the changes they make. I don't think anyone who has genuinely struggled with their mental health would claim that a single change could fix everything.

Diet matters, exercise matters, sleep matters, thinking matters; EVERYTHING matters. And that's precisely why no one thing is THE solution. No single issue in your life is causing your problems, so no single change will fix them.

People who claim to offer a quick and simple solution don't consider the damage this does. They don't understand that you're going to blame and shame yourself when you follow their instructions and only feel a little bit better, or don't notice any improvement whatsoever. They don't care that their failure to live up to their promises reinforces your belief that you're broken, damaged, and unfixable.

I know it isn't that easy. I understand that there is no one skill I can teach you, no single statement I can make to you that will create a significant dent in your pain. That's why I'm going to teach you a little bit of everything. I'll cover the foundational elements of all of the tools that I use in my day to help the people I work with and everything that helped me dig myself out of that hole.

We have to be honest about what you're up against. We don't all enter this existence with equal opportunity for joy and success. Most mental health conditions have significant genetic components, meaning they begin to take shape before a person is even born. Some of us simply have to work much harder for our happiness than others. Mental health is not a level playing field. Please be so wary of anyone who promises quick or simple fixes for the almost incomprehensible complexities of being human.

I promise that I'm just as frustrated as you are

Professional mental health is a lottery.

I've worked with providers who believe that nobody gets better, even though I see evidence to the contrary every day. I've heard stories of providers getting frustrated with their clients and telling them, "I can't help you." I constantly hear about people who are forced to retell their trauma stories over and over again while given no assistance or training on how to stay regulated while doing so. Many "professionals" have nothing to offer you besides a kind and empathic ear and empty, meaningless guidance like "think positive" or "visualize good things happening to you."

When I see the help that's available for those who are struggling, I mostly feel embarrassed. Embarrassed that this is all we have to offer you. Embarassed that this is as far as we've managed to come. It feels so inadequate to me.

Please don't let the shortcomings of contemporary mental health treatments allow you to believe that you're the problem. Our absolute gold standard treatments, the most efficacious therapeutic techniques and psychiatric medications, help about 50% of people who seek treatment. Half. We help half of the people who come to us, and we consider that a massive success. The half who doesn't benefit is often explained away as being "treatment resistant," "difficult clients," or "willful."

If you've had any of these experiences, I want to say something to you on behalf of the entire field of mental health. It's not you who have failed; it's us. You came to us during a dark time in your life, you were vulnerable and open, and we didn't give you what you needed. I am so, so very sorry about that. It means everything to me that you're willing to keep trying.

Your promise

There's one thing I'd like to ask you to promise me before we leave the introduction. I want you to promise that you will genuinely attempt this work. Read this book as a participant, not as a spectator. This work, in a way, is a relationship between the two of us. I'm putting everything I know into the blank space that exists between us and offering it to you. I can't make you take these words and accept them into your world. Only you can decide to do that.

I don't want you to just read my words and think, "wow, that's interesting," and then go about your life as it previously was, unless you're delighted with your life as-is and are just reading this out of curiosity. I think something drew you here. You have a lot of options when it comes to self-help books, and you chose this one. That means something.

I was very meticulous about the design and appearance of this book. You saw this cover, saw the title, read a few words on the back or the first page, and you felt something. It may have been momentary, but you felt something. Something you don't often feel. Perhaps it was understanding, or validation, or hope, or a feeling you can't quite name. But it was there. That's why you're still reading.

The worst thing you can do is approach this half-heartedly. Being caught partway between accepting life as it currently is and wanting to change it gives you the worst of both worlds. You'll be aware enough of your dissatisfaction to be bothered by it, but won't be committed enough to improve it. It's a life of emotional purgatory.

I don't want this to happen to you, which is why I'm asking this promise of you. Put your entire being into our time together. Your whole heart and soul. Don't dip a toe into the water of change and see if it helps. It won't, because what you're up against doesn't do half-measures. You need to match its intensity. If you want to see real progress, I need you all in. Can you promise me that you'll try?

VAPOR PART 2

You haven't been forgotten about.
The world is holding a place for you.
It's OK if you haven't found it yet.
But I promise it's out there somewhere.
Waiting to be discovered.
Everything here has a place.
Every blade of grass, every grain of sand.
Every bird, every fish, every insect, every mammal.
We are all part of a great process.
And that includes you.
You may feel abandoned.
You may feel left behind.
But you haven't been forgotten.
We're waiting for you to step into the light.
To be the person only you can be.
Beautiful, Powerful, Unique, Special.
The brokenness you feel is artificial.
It's an illusion created by pain and shame.
And reinforced by the walls you built to protect yourself.
Try to let those walls come down a little today.
I know you think they protect you.
But mostly, they just isolate you.
Your place isn't behind walls, locks, or gates.
It isn't in a dark room by yourself.
It's out here with the rest of us.
You belong here as much as anyone.
And you always have.
Please find your place in this world.

Without you here, the world has a piece missing.
You are loved more than you can know.

PART II: THE LIES

"The strength of a belief doesn't measure the accuracy of the belief. It only measures the frequency with which that belief has been repeated."

THE SIX LIES THE WORLD TELLS YOU

Why do we devalue ourselves every day? Why do we find it so hard to offer the patience, compassion, and empathy to ourselves that we can usually hold for others? Why are we so easily convinced of our flaws, our brokenness, our unlovability?

Because we listen to lies.

There are six of them in particular that impact everyone I've worked with in therapy to some extent. I've come to regard them as universal human struggles. Almost all of us go about our lives believing these lies, living and making decisions in accordance with them. They become heavier and heavier each day, crushing our spirits, grinding us into submission. They take away our vibrance, our passion, and our drive and leave us with hopelessness, discouragement, and exhaustion in their place. They are mostly unseen and unacknowledged. They are relentless, omnipresent, and unimaginably destructive.

These lies will wear you down to nothing if you don't catch them and speak truth to them. They can take everything from you. They convince you to accept the unacceptable. They drag you so far away from who you began this journey as that you don't even recognize yourself anymore. You will never be who you want to be and can't possibly feel how you want to feel as long as they dictate your life.

First, you have to learn to identify them. They don't present themselves as lies. They present themselves as factual, objective truths. Others around you have accepted them, live by them, and repeat them, making them appear that much more real. You see them on television shows, hear them in conversations, read them in books meant for children. They're "normal" thoughts and feelings. Once you learn to identify them, you'll start to see them everywhere.

Next, you have to learn to respond to them. To speak the truth back to them. The lies don't whisper to you. They shout, they yell, and they scream. They don't take days off, and they're everywhere. The only way you can take ground back from them is to match their intensity. Take all of the anger, frustration, and disillusionment that you typically bottle up and use it. Every urge to defy, every silenced critique gets to have a voice now.

I'll tell you what I say to them. Think of my responses as templates; feel free to use them as-is if that's your preference, but think about adjusting them to make them your own. Your responses will feel more believable and authentic if they sound like they're coming from you.

We're going to address the guilt and the shame, the regret, and the self-judgment that drags you down every day by helping you realize that you did not make yourself this way. The finger you constantly point at yourself for all your shortcomings, all your imperfections, and all your mistakes is guided by assumptions and oversimplifications. The truth about how you ended up here is so much more complicated than "I made some bad choices." Inappropriate self-blame will drag you down to the core of this earth and keep you trapped there as long as you listen to it.

We're going to talk about the feelings of helplessness and powerlessness, that constant sensation of being at the mercy of a callous world, and why it's not quite so dire as it seems. Right now, you're being guided by an invisible neurological hand to walk a hidden behavioral path. Once you learn how to see that hand and travel the other pathways, you gain unimaginable freedom. You have such incredible power over your own life if you learn how to use it. You know more about yourself than all of the other 7.7 billion people on this planet combined know about you.

We're going to work on the loneliness and the longing, the sense that you're incomplete or hollow, by helping you find what already lives inside of you. What you've been searching for so desperately has been hiding in plain sight all along. Waiting for you to discover it, love it, nurture it. You have something in your possession right this very moment that's more valuable than anything you've been searching for in this world, and it's ready to be found.

We're going to help you finally get some distance from those nagging, repetitive, inherently negative thoughts that plague you nonstop. The ones that tell you "you aren't good enough" or "your needs don't matter." The ones you know are wrong but can't stop listening to, like a vapid but catchy pop song. Your life is governed every day by rules that aren't real, by facts that aren't true. You listen to directions you can't hear and don't even realize you're doing it most of the time. These rules and facts are nothing more than the ideas you've listened to the most frequently. Once you understand how these ideas get in your head, you can override them with new truths.

We're going to deal with the crippling stress and the debilitating sensation of being chronically overwhelmed by getting rid of all your pointless measuring sticks. You cannot get where you want to be through sheer willpower and effort alone. Trying to get out of this rut by pushing yourself as hard as possible as often as possible is like thrashing after you've fallen through the ice on a lake. All it will do is break your footholds until you either drown or freeze to death. There's a way out of that cold, cold water, and it's so much simpler than it seems.

We're going to talk about how waiting to feel ready for something is an evolutionary failure, an outdated security mechanism. Almost nothing is as scary, as threatening, or as complicated as it appears to your mind. Your brain is not always your ally. It wants you to be safe far more than it wants you to be happy.

You might have some big feelings in this section. Moments of anger, frustration, fear, and confusion. There's a lot to unravel, and realizing you've been misled is an unpleasant experience. Take your time working through this section. Take breaks if you need to. You're entitled to every reaction you experience.

THE TREE

I sat under the tree when my heart was broken.
I sat under the tree when I had nothing left.
I sat under the tree when I felt like I was disappearing.
I sat under the tree when I knew there was a life out there, somewhere, that I was supposed to be living.
I sat under the tree when I realized I was never going to find that life.
Somehow, the tree seemed to absorb it all.
I always felt some measure of relief, if only briefly.
Like so many things in my life, one day the tree was just gone.
Cut down by someone unknown person.
Probably just doing their job.
Unaware it meant anything to anyone.
Or that it meant the world to one person.
I'm probably the only person alive who ever cared about that tree.
People don't tend to understand what's special to me.
Or why I care as much as I do.
Every now and then, I find little retreats.
Spaces where I feel safe and comfortable.
Until someone cuts them down with a chainsaw.

LIE #1: EVERYTHING IS YOUR FAULT

When we fall short, when we struggle, or when we fail, we suddenly manage to forget everything we know about ourselves. We strip away our knowledge of our past, our circumstances, and our inner experience. Within this complete vacuum of context, we judge ourselves as if we were looking at a stranger. A stranger who we inexplicably don't like very much.

We're unwilling to accept any deviations or missteps in our journey. We expect the world from ourselves while expecting nothing from the world. This creates a dangerous, damaging, insidious internal reaction. I found it last night in a children's book I was reading to my daughter.

The main character was a girl in elementary school who spends her morning daydreaming about school lunch. Her favorite food is on the menu today. On her way to the cafeteria, she trips and hurts herself. She misses part of the lunch period because she has to visit the school nurse after her fall. When she finally arrives at the cafeteria, the food service worker mishears her order because the room is too loud and gives her the wrong food. Her daydream is over. What she wanted most from this day, a simple request for a favorite food, is now out of reach.

She makes her way to her lunch table, visibly disappointed and drained, but the period ends just after she sits down. She doesn't get to eat anything, not even the consolation prize of a meal she was given. She spends the rest of her school day hungry and disappointed. Nobody comforts her or validates her. Nobody apologizes for what happened. Nobody even notices her pain.

Rather than playing or relaxing after school, she spends most of her evening making a plan. A plan to make sure she gets the proper lunch tomorrow and has time to eat it. Her plan is to execute each part of her morning to perfection so that the incredibly flawed system she is forced to navigate doesn't prevent her from meeting her basic physiological needs. Miraculously, she pulls it off. She dodges every land mine of her elementary school life and succeeds in eating lunch that day. According to the summary on the back of the book this was a fun adventure, a tale of resilience and problem-solving, a story of success.

This is a story of failure. It's the story of a little girl whose needs are missed by everyone around her. The tale of invisible and unvalidated emotions leading to an internal dissociation from emotion. It's a tale about existing within a dysfunctional system that is indifferent to your existence, of walking cavernous hallways and sitting in immense lunchrooms full of peers and adults yet somehow being alone. It's the story of all of our lives.

We're supposed to like this story? We're supposed to feel good about how it ended? We aren't supposed to be disturbed by the fact that nobody expressed a hint of empathy or validation over a little girl having a terrible day and not getting to eat? The systems in place didn't work, and nobody fixed the systems. And that's supposed to be acceptable to us.

These are the messages being programmed into us from day one. The expectation is that we all know how to do this. Navigate whatever broken systems you have to navigate by yourself. Show no distress, no "weakness," no feelings at all, or you invite attacks. Never criticize the system. Only blame yourself for not fitting into the system. The world is blameless; you are responsible for everything wrong in your life.

I want you to start rejecting this message. After all, you didn't even choose to exist. You were created without your consent by people you had never met. Your brain was designing itself, crafting your personality traits, sketching pathways of thought, and setting the range of your emotional sensitivity before you were even born. You had no awareness of these processes, no option to make any changes to them. Then came your birth, upon which your physical safety and emotional health were placed in the hands of total strangers when you were the most vulnerable and helpless version of yourself. They might have loved you. They might have wanted you. They might have been prepared for you. Or they might not have been any of those things. If they weren't, nobody could protect you from that.

The world then began to shape you against your will. You had experiences that you didn't choose, many of which were unpleasant and unwanted. You went to schools that were selected for you. You lived in a neighborhood that was selected for you. During your day, you were surrounded by people randomly thrown into the same arbitrary life circumstances as you. People who influenced you, molded you. You started to mimic them, sometimes out of necessity to avoid being teased or excluded. Because you were a child with minimal critical thinking skills, you couldn't discern the bad ideas from the good ideas; you took everything in with no filter, no vetting of concepts and rules. You soaked up beliefs, arbitrary norms and regulations, behavioral patterns, communication styles, and everything else you were exposed to.

You emerge from this broken system with scars, wounds, and damage. Damage you may have never been taught to repair. Damage that makes you feel angry, hopeless, defensive, and fearful. When you show these feelings to the world, hoping for understanding and empathy, you receive shame and judgment. You are blamed for being changed by a life you didn't choose.

I'm over it. I am completely 100% over the brokenness we are expected to accept every day when we can be rejected for the slightest flaw or mistake. I am absolutely sick and tired of being expected to have a positive relationship with a narcissistic, gaslighting mess of a society. And if you feel the same, I'll accept that from you even if nobody else will. Because I think you're doing your absolute best, even when it doesn't look like it on the outside.

I think this world has been horrible to you at times and that the world itself holds much of the responsibility for where your life is today. You've experienced things you should never have experienced, things you had no way to avoid. You've been asked to overcome challenges that nobody bothered to teach you how to overcome. Those things still matter to you and still impact you, even if they're functionally over and done with. Your life has been a group project, not a solo assignment. Trying to pin all of this on you is a fallacy. It's an oversimplified scapegoating of epic proportions for an almost incomprehensibly complicated problem.

I don't think that anyone has ever really taken the time to teach you the skills you've needed to manage your life. I don't believe that anyone has consistently given you the reassurance and validation you needed to hear. I think you were thrown straight into this chaos and expected to thrive. If I'm right about these things, your self-blame won't hold up very well when we yank it from the shameful shadows it hides in and hold it up into the light of reality. It's not fair to expect someone to be great at something if they were never given the proper tools to do it.

Your formal education was focused on rote learning. You were required to memorize and reiterate a blend of practical skills and trivial information. Many of the people who taught you didn't care about you, and some of them didn't even want to be there. The requirements for knowing how to take care of yourself were minimal. You had a health class here and there. You played sports in gym class. A group of people with doctorate degrees decided that was all you needed. It was assumed that the rest of the knowledge you needed to function would come from family and friends.

You were handed the freedom to make dangerous, destructive, life-altering choices based on your chronological age, not on how much guidance you were given about the consequences of those choices. At some point it was decided that, going forward, you were fully responsible for your own wellbeing. There weren't any established criteria used to determine when this shift happened. Nobody knows exactly what makes someone ready to be a healthy adult. Sometimes people "officially" become adults for no other reason than the adults who had been taking care of them didn't feel like doing it anymore. We're legally able to decide almost everything for ourselves at 18 years old, even though our brains don't reach physical maturity until age 25.

Some of us have to try to learn impulse control from addicts. Some of us have to try to learn stress management from burnt-out workaholics. Some of us have to learn how to have healthy relationships from people who can't talk to each other. Some of us have to try to learn how to have a healthy relationship with our bodies from people who hate the way they look. Broken. System.

We're asked to trust that the people in charge will do the right thing, even though we know from psychology's dark past that people will abuse and electrocute one another and feel justified in doing so if instructed to by an authority figure. We're told to send our children to places where we aren't in control without guiding them even though we know that humans are dangerous and unpredictable. We know that what children need most from their parents is love and nurturing, yet parents forego providing love and nurturing to secure more resources. There's a disconnect between what we know about people and what we expect people to do.

All of our systems fail people. Our family systems fail people. Our education system fails people. Our healthcare system fails people. Our design for creating healthy adults is a failure. You're at the mercy of whatever ecosystem you're dropped into, and it's just assumed that this will work for you. It works for some people, some of the time. But it fails so many.

We are all the products of this failed system. Consequences of being innocent, naïve, and vulnerable and being faced with chaos, unpredictability, and illogical and arbitrary rules. Products of trying to understand the difference between the way things seem like they should be and the way they are, trying our best to make sense of the senseless.

Being a person is incredibly confusing and frustrating. In many ways, we don't work the way it seems like we should. How many of these have happened to you?

- Getting insomnia from trying hard to fall asleep
- Loving someone so intensely it pushed them away
- Trying so hard not to think about something that you can't stop thinking about it
- Becoming more nervous or stressed out because you avoided something that made you anxious
- Failing at something because you worked too hard at it
- Being just as worn out after taking a break as you were before the break
- Getting stuck in a grieving process because you pushed through the pain

That's how much sense we make. Try your hardest at something, and sometimes you get the complete opposite. We're unintuitive creatures in so many ways. We don't need contradictory folk wisdom and inconsistent role models. We need operating manuals.

Maybe someone noticed your struggles and helped connect you with professional support. Hope you lucked out and found one of the good ones and not one of the burnt-out, passionless, or incompetent ones. Mental health is a young field. Even the best of us don't always know how to help people. Contemporary mental health informed by psychological and behavioral research has only existed for about 100 years. That's nothing in the world of science. A hundred years into cancer treatment, we were still tying bags of plant matter to people's bodies to heal them.

Do you still think it's all your fault? Do you really have a solid counter-argument to everything I've said here? Because I've been searching for one my whole life, and I don't feel like I've found it. I can't find the logic behind the self-blame. I don't think it's there.

I think you've been swimming against the current, doing your best with whatever you were given, even if what you were given was pathetically inadequate. And that's precisely why I still have hope for you. So much hope. Challenging this message of inappropriate self-blame is how we start to take back your mind. It belongs to you, and we're going to do our best not to let anyone abuse or manipulate it anymore. I want you to practice rejecting the blame and guilt the world tries to place upon you for its problems. I want you to realize the truth of how you got here, the objective unfairness of what's been asked of you. Most importantly, I want you to remember that this isn't all your fault.

Remember This:

When you catch yourself shaming, blaming, or judging yourself to an unreasonable degree, respond to the lie with a statement like:

"I'm still working through the effects of events

I didn't choose to experience."

THE TREE PART 2

Stop assuming that the problem lies with you.
It's more likely that the world has failed you.
This world sells you on promises, and then it breaks them.
It promises that everything works out eventually, no matter what.
It promises that when the time comes, you will be ready.
It promises that you will automatically know how to live, how to be, how to thrive.
It promises lies.
We don't instinctually know how to live.
We aren't all given equal opportunity.
We are often unprepared for what comes next.
We are thrown into this immense meat grinder of a world and just expected to survive.
I believe that you are doing your best, even if you are so far away from your dreams that you can't even see them anymore.
Because I know all of this, I know there is still hope.
You've been doing what you can with what you have.
What happens if you have more?
What if you knew the truth about how your mind works?
What if you knew how to cope effectively with the worst that this world can throw at you?
What if, instead of constantly walking through a forest in the dark, you had a guide with a light?
Someone who has already walked this trail.
Someone who knows the way.
If you knew where I came from, you would know that anything is possible.

That nobody can venture to the point of no return.
If you knew all this, do you think you would see your dreams again?
I think you will.
Take my hand.
Stand up.
We can plant more trees together.
We'll water them and watch them grow.
We'll give them the nurturing they need.
And we won't let anyone cut them down this time.

LIE #2: YOU CAN'T CHANGE ANYTHING

I had all kinds of ideas for a way out. My favorite was knighthood. In my mind, I spent hours of my days living in Europe during the middle ages. There was something magnetically appealing about how simple that life sounded to me. I loved the idea that if I was talented enough with a sword or a bow, I could find a role in the world regardless of what anyone thought of me. I just wanted to scour the countryside for threats to my kingdom and protect the people I loved. I would have traded my life for that in a heartbeat, even with the plagues and food insecurities.

What's your ideal way out? Maybe, like me, you dream about being born in the past, a particular era where you feel you would have fit in better. Perhaps you dream about being born into the future, into an unknown that seems like it could only be preferable to this mess. Maybe you wish you were born in a different country or into another family. Perhaps you simply wish you could change the world so that you could finally feel at home in it.

I know how powerless this life can feel. The people in charge are so different and detached from most of us. We're told to live by laws and rules created by rulers and lawmakers who have never met us. Our social norms are handed down from generation to generation, created by people whose lifestyles are incomprehensible to us. There's something frustratingly distant and detached about our social power structure. It can be an awkward, confusing mess, and it's so normal to want to be able to change the world or find an escape from it.

The thing is, you can change the world. Even though you can't time travel or rewrite your personal history, you can redefine how you experience the events that shape your life to an extent. It's a change that comes from within, and it's more powerful than you can imagine.

There are two worlds that you experience. There is an objective "real world" that exists outside of all of us. We can all influence it, some of us more than others, but none of us can truly control it. It is a shared product of all of humanity in combination with factors that none of us control or even understand. You can't change that world. You can't even fully experience that world. None of us can.

The second world lives inside of you. This world impacts you so much more than the first world does. Even though the objective real world is the source of most stimuli, your experience of that stimuli is internal. Your nervous system processes the stimuli provided by the first world and sends signals to your brain for interpretation. Your brain then uses them to create the second world. Technically, everything you experience only happens inside of you. Your world is synaptic activity, electrical transmission between neurons. It's your own private ecosystem.

The actual, objective outer world and your inner experience of this world differ in so many ways. What color is this book? White, or light gray, with black text, right? Your perception of those colors only exists inside of you. We don't know what the actual colors of objects in our environment are, or if they even have colors. Your experience of objects having specific colors is created by your retinas absorbing light reflections and sending sensory signals to your brain for processing. The colors you see are a simulation of a visual experience. They only exist in your perception, your world. The objective external world is something else entirely, something you will never accurately know.

You can change your inner world. It's already changing constantly, with or without your guidance. You are a dynamic creature, a constant work in progress. No matter what happens outside of you, your mind will always belong to you. You are the author of your narrative, not the world.

Your nervous system changes over time, and your interpretation of stimuli changes with it. That's why your subjective tastes aren't static across your lifespan. Music that once sounded pleasant to your ears becomes grating, and vice versa. You learn to enjoy different foods, and in turn, lose interest in other foods. Each of these shifts changes our inner world.

The predictions you make about what your future life looks like and your choices about handling various life situations are primarily based on your memories. As you continue your existence in this world, you form new memories. New memories create new predictions and new choices. This changes your inner world.

I'm not saying that you can consistently change pleasure into pain or despair into hope. Sometimes that works, and sometimes it doesn't. I'm not saying that life is all mind over matter or that positive thinking changes everything. This is about consciously and intentionally rearranging your internal architecture. It won't eliminate all of your suffering, it won't cure your trauma, but it can take away at least some of your pain. I think that's worth doing.

You have access to more information about yourself than you could fit in an entire public library. You only give voice to a tiny fraction of the thoughts, emotions, and memories you experience in a day. Not even the people closest to you understand what it's like to be you. The world doesn't know you. Nothing it does to you is personal. Only you know you. So many of your daily decisions come from your deepest insecurities, your most painful memories, and your secret goals and dreams you don't dare to voice. You have access to all of your classified documents. You are the world's leading expert on you, and you always will be.

Your internal systems are more complicated than a nuclear reactor. Your brain is the most powerful, beautiful, and remarkable possession you will ever own. It contains roughly 100,000,000,000 neurons, or brain cells. That's almost one neuron for every dollar Jeff Bezos has (note: this was accurate when I first wrote this section. Bezos has really pulled ahead during the COVID-19 pandemic. Freaking Bezos.) (2021 note: Freaking Musk).

It's hard to conceptualize the immensity of your cognition without a visual aid. Imagine a field a million acres in size. You stand in the middle of it, and it stretches beyond your visible range in every direction. Every few seconds, a flower blooms. These flowers have different shapes, various sizes, and come in every color imaginable. Over time, the landscape of this field can look dramatically different depending on which flowers are blooming. You aren't the creator of this garden. You are the gardener. You choose which seeds to plant, which to water, and which flowers to pull. The field will never look exactly the way you want it to. It's too immense to micromanage to that degree, but you do influence it. You are anything but powerless.

This is why you're the hero of your story. You're plugged into yourself 24/7. Every thought, every action, every belief, every dream is something you have at least a degree of freedom in. You can care for yourself in ways that nobody else ever could because you know about wants and needs that you never voice. You can resolve internal distress before you even have time to speak it. Your speed, your power, and your knowledge in the context of your life are unprecedented, supernatural. You are the ruler of your internal kingdom.

Don't misunderstand this. You can't directly force your

mind to think happy thoughts or to be optimistic about the future any more than you can directly force your heart to slow down or your kidneys to speed up. There's latency between your generation of thought and your awareness of thought. Just a few milliseconds, but it's not quite real-time. Your awareness of everything that happens inside you lives ever so slightly in the past. In other words, by the time you realize your mind is drifting towards a particular topic, it's already there. It's too late to stop it.

Want an example? Whatever you do right now, under no circumstances should you allow yourself to think about a black cat.

What happened? Did you briefly visualize a black cat, then quickly try to suppress it? You have to think about something to tell yourself not to think about it. Yet another cognitive paradox.

Despite your lack of complete, real-time control over your thought process, your power is still immense. You can change the world inside of yourself so that it's uniquely suited for you to inhabit. Your own precious, unique sanctuary from all of this madness. Whatever you lack from your environment, please give it to yourself. Nobody has empathy for your situation? Give yourself all the compassion you have. Everyone is impatient with you? Practice patience with yourself. People are mad at you? Show yourself tolerance and understanding. Give yourself everything the world failed to provide you with.

If you doubt the power of changing your inner world, there's no better example to prove my point than death. When you die, your inner world dies with you. All of your thoughts, feelings, memories, and beliefs cease to exist. Your experience of this world ends completely, yet this world continues to exist for everyone else.

Don't let yourself be tricked into thinking you're helpless. Never lose awareness of your incredible power. Remind yourself of it whenever you feel lost, hopeless, or defeated. Continue speaking these truths to yourself. It will feel fake at first, like you're an actor rehearsing lines for a play. Over time, you'll start to believe in them and learn how to use them. Once that happens, everything changes.

Remember This:

For the most part, your life happens inside of you. You have minimal influence on the outside world, but tremendous influence on your inner world. When you're feeling helpless or powerless, remind yourself of something like this:

"The person who has the most control over my life is me."

3 AM

Why don't I sleep anymore?
Everyone else has been asleep for hours.
I used to sleep.
I don't understand what happened.
I can't handle the quiet anymore.
The quieter the world.
The louder my mind.
Night is just too quiet.
It makes my brain scream.
I tried to sleep in the furnace room.
Every time the furnace motor kicked on, my mind quieted somewhat.
It gave me little moments of almost-peace.
The hum of the machine soothing me.
I found comfort in the muted roar of the flame inside.
Something about it reminded me of myself.
Then it would shut off.
And every thought came rushing back with the silence.
Wide awake once again.
It was like that all night.
On/Off.
Calm/Losing my mind.
Why is it that everyone but me can rest?
Their lives are all just as screwed up as mine.
Yet they're sleeping peacefully, recharging themselves for the next round.
While I'm staring at water-damaged ceiling tiles.
Wondering if I'll ever really sleep again.

The way I used to before all of this began.

LIE #3: SOMETHING IS MISSING

I know you feel like a half-finished creation sometimes. A rough draft of a person, a template of a human. I also know that you're not.

I'm sure you want an explanation for why everyone except you seems satisfied, resilient, and at peace while you have to scratch and claw for even a hint of excitement, joy, or contentment. You can look like them, but it's just a mask you wear. It doesn't accurately reflect your internal reality. You want to feel the way they seem to feel. I don't blame you. It's a miserable feeling to think you're on the other side of a ravine from everybody else and that there's no bridge to cross that gap.

It's tempting to let yourself become fixated on the differences between yourself and others. They're right in front of you, easy to identify and analyze. Maybe it seems like if you lost weight, made more money, had a partner, had a better partner, had kids, or didn't have kids, you would finally find your "missing piece." But have you noticed that the missing piece keeps changing? You probably have some of your previous missing pieces in your life right now, yet here you are with the same incomplete, half-empty feeling.

All of those things can make a difference, but the most significant difference between the people who are legitimately at ease with life most of the time and the people who seldom feel that way isn't something you can see by looking at them. It's something inside of them. People can have everything they've ever dreamed of but still feel empty. People can also have none of these things and still be content. What is outside of you cannot heal what is wounded inside of you.

I've worked with people of every different background and life situation that you can imagine. There's only one variable I've ever found that consistently separates "happy" people from "unhappy" people; the quality of their relationship with themselves.

Every morning you wake up with a key in your hand. The key unlocks acceptance, understanding, and love. It opens a chest of appreciation for yourself, a sense of wholeness, completeness, and joy. Every morning, you throw this key in a dumpster. Then you go looking for it, everywhere except the place you threw it.

The most precious thing you have in this world, your most sacred possession, is yourself. It is so, so easy to miss this. We value things based mainly on how novel they are and how important we're told that they are. We assume one product is better than another because it costs more. We presume one artist is better than another because they have more plays, views, or sales. And most of us are told, over and over again in so many different ways, that we aren't special. Another lie.

Grammy award-winning violinist Joshua Bell once played a one-hour concert in a subway, unannounced and anonymous, on a violin worth over $3,000,000. Of the thousands of people that passed him, exactly six stopped to listen. Six. Less than 0.1%. Most people didn't realize they were walking past something special. They were distracted by their thoughts, their lives, their distress, and their inner worlds.

In another context, people would have paid thousands of dollars to watch this performance. It was the environment that hid the true, spectacular nature of what most of them walked right past. This is you every day. You're a 3-million-dollar violin in a dark, dirty subway, a world-class violinist with a distracted, impassionate audience. You pass by something extraordinary, incredible, and magical nearly every second of every day. Your missing piece. Yourself.

You treat yourself like you're less than others. You act as if you're less deserving of your time, energy, patience, and compassion than those around you. The best you have to offer is reserved for other people, and you get whatever scraps are left. Many days, there isn't anything left over. I want that to end today. It's time for you to rejoin the ranks of the people that matter to you. You were there once, and you can be there again.

How would you treat yourself if you achieved tremendous fame? If you were world-renowned for whatever it is that you do? Recognized everywhere you went, followed by millions on social media? Would you carry yourself with more pride? Would you think and speak differently? Would you be less willing to accept poor treatment from others?

The only difference between the fantasy of this famous version of yourself and the person you are today is other people's perspectives. Nothing about you in this scenario has been changed from the present, real version of yourself. You're just you, but you are celebrated by others for being you. This validation, this social proof, changes your experience and your internal perspective of yourself. That was the only difference between Joshua Bell in the subway and Joshua Bell in a concert hall; perspective. The difference in response was profound.

There's a difference between being special to the world and being special to yourself. The world may never regard you as important, but that doesn't need to hold you back from seeing it. You don't have to wait for other people to appreciate you in order to appreciate yourself. Society will probably never celebrate you for the miracle that you are. Even if it does, that fame is often fleeting. Why allow other people to determine your worth, your value, and the quality of your life? Haven't they done enough of that already?

I want you to take the responsibility of assessing your value out of the hands of other people and place it back into your own. After all, nobody else is more qualified. No other person bears witness to the bloody warfare that takes place in your mind every day. Nobody but you can celebrate the hundreds of unseen and unspoken victories you claim over your darkest thoughts and feelings. Only one person can see all of this. How do you think you'll feel if that person ignores all of it?

There's nothing missing inside of you, even if it feels like there is. You were born a complete, whole being. That has never changed. It cannot change. The world can beat you down in so many ways, but one thing it can never do is remove your wholeness. There is no mechanism for taking it out of you. You're still here, just as much as you always have been. You might just be buried under the habits, beliefs, and desires this world has instilled upon you.

Nobody can be more or less important than any other person. If I put you in front of a jury right this very second and asked you to prove that you objectively matter less than someone else, could you do it? What would you say? That you've made mistakes? That you've hurt people? That you've failed? Do you think those things make you unique? Those experiences don't set you apart from humanity; they make you a part of humanity. What is so different about you, specifically, that allows you to justify having a separate set of rules for yourself than you do for everybody else? If you look at yourself and your life without your biases, I think you'll find that the answer is "nothing."

You're the only person who can promise never to leave you. You're the only person who is capable of truly understanding your heart and your mind. You are your soul mate. The depth of your relationship with yourself cannot be matched by your relationship with anyone else. Nothing in your life, no person, no situation, no relationship will have anywhere close to the impact on your life that you have on your life. If your relationship with yourself isn't in a good place, your life will feel like there's an invisible magnet beneath you that continually sucks the good out of things. Every exciting and joyful moment will be blunted. Every opportunity will be tainted by doubt. Lacking a healthy relationship with yourself leaves a void inside of you. A person cannot thrive within a void.

The void will grow and grow until you do something about it. Our world is full of things designed to help distract you from the void. Using drugs or alcohol excessively, immersive video games, social media, unhealthy relationships, workaholism, and so much more. Most consumer products are designed at least in part to distract us from loneliness and unhappiness. To help us pretend that void isn't there. To make us feel whole and well, at least for a little bit.

It doesn't work, and you know it doesn't work, but you keep trying anyway because it helps for a while, and you think that's the best you can get. It isn't. You can fill that void, but there's only one thing that can fill it for more than a few hours; improving the quality of your relationship with yourself. Leveling up the only guaranteed constant in your daily life. To get there, you'll need a lot more than a yoga class and a nice warm cup of coffee here and there. Those can certainly be elements of self-care, but they're only a tiny fraction of what you need to heal this relationship.

If another person were constantly insulting you, dragging you down, and second-guessing you, they can't just take you out to a fancy dinner and call it good, right? They have to show consistent remorse, growth, and change. They have to continually prioritize you, focus on you, and pay attention to you to work on healing the damage they've done if they want to stay in your life. If you're going to heal your relationship with yourself, you have to apply these same principles. You have to be all in for yourself, and it has to be consistent.

Your single most important job in this world is to become exceptionally good at taking care of yourself. I believe this is a universal human truth no matter what you do for a living, what your spiritual beliefs are, or how many people depend on you. I believe that the more people rely on you, the more critical your self-care becomes.

Without healthy and effective self-care, your foundation will crumble under stress. You won't be able to continue doing all of the wonderful things you have done or want to do in your life. You'll become stuck and stagnant, frustrated and disappointed. No matter how strong, driven, or resilient a person is, nobody can function at a high level indefinitely without recharging. The world has done a great job of shaping you to take excellent care of it, but not of yourself. We need to change this.

Nobody can do it for you. Your self-care is your job and your responsibility. How well you do this job impacts everyone around you tremendously. Do people get the healthy, vibrant, energetic version of you? Or do they get the exhausted, burnt out, just-trying-to-make-it-to-tomorrow version of you? They want the former. Learning to take proper care of yourself is the most selfless thing you can do.

Have you ever witnessed someone else's downward spiral? Watched the inevitable fall, knowing they could stop it but that you can't make them stop it? Having your feelings entirely at the mercy of whether someone else decided to take care of themselves or not? There's nothing quite like it, and that's what you'll eventually inflict upon your loved ones if you refuse to take care of yourself. Putting others first and chronically neglecting your own needs is selfish. What other people need most from you is for you to practice adequate self-care because nobody else can do that for you.

If you're convinced yourself that you don't need or deserve affection, validation, time, love, or any other unavoidable human need, you're practicing reverse narcissism. A narcissist believes they're more important than everyone else and should be treated with special care and rules. You believe you're less important than everyone else and should be treated with special care and rules. Same logic, opposite direction.

If you want to consistently feel complete and whole, practice treasuring yourself, valuing yourself, savoring yourself, and prizing yourself. Take all of that time and energy you typically spend chasing all of the worldly things you've been told are the missing pieces in your life and reinvest them internally. Use the key that only you hold instead of throwing it away and then looking for it in other places. Give yourself everything that this existence has thus far failed to provide for you. Do your best to never forget your wholeness. Don't let the world convince you that something is missing from inside of you. It profits off of your longing, your misery, your false beliefs. Like a manipulative partner, it wants you to struggle so that you need something from it. What you need most resides only in you.

Remember This:

Nothing will impact the quality of your life as much as your relationship with yourself. If you neglect this relationship to pursue other things, you'll never experience the joy, the peace, and the wholeness that you're chasing. When you find yourself feeling incomplete, lacking, empty, or like you're missing something, remind yourself of something like this:

"I am a complete being, and most of what
I need lives within me."

3 AM PART 2

Your mind is overwhelmed.
It's tired of trying to make sense of the senseless.
It's constantly processing, "screaming" at you, because it's being asked to do too much.
It's a bit more aware of certain things than most people's minds.
More bothered by what many can let go of.
Or hide from.
Nobody is taking care of it.
It shouldn't be your job already.
But the people around you aren't equipped to do it.
Everybody's mind is complicated.
But yours is a little extra.
I know that, right now, that makes you miserable.
But someday, you will use it to do great things.
And someday, you will sleep again.
But it might be a while.

LIE #4: WHAT FEELS TRUE IS TRUE

You're living in captivity. Right this very moment, you exist within a prison. You can't see it or feel it, but it restricts you nonetheless. You perceive boundaries and walls that don't exist. Arbitrary, subjective rules dictate your thoughts, beliefs, and choices.

Sometimes animals are raised in captivity and then released into the wild. The transition is dramatic, and it doesn't always go well. Sometimes the animals are so habituated to living in restricted environments that they don't know how to handle freedom. They pace around their new natural environment in the same movement patterns they were restricted to when they lived in a cage. They aren't able to recognize that the walls which once constrained them aren't there anymore.

We aren't so different. We spend the vast majority of our formative years in two environments; school and home. Each setting has a specific set of rules. Sometimes the laws in one environment contradict the rules in the other. Sometimes "home" is more than one place, and each home has different rules. We learn and generally follow the rules because unpleasant things happen to us if we don't. At some point our environment expands beyond school and home, and we're released into the world thinking we understand the rules of life.

Inevitably, we encounter situations we aren't prepared for. Experiences where the rules we know don't apply or don't work. We see other people living by different rules. We face the reality that what we thought were universal laws of human functioning were nothing more than the subjective beliefs of the adults we were randomly assigned to.

You can learn things that aren't true. The degree to which you believe something is based so much more on how often you've heard it than on how much sense it makes. The rules you currently live your life by were formed by repeated exposure to other people's perspectives and beliefs. In other words, you aren't totally "you." The way you think, feel, and act, the values you hold, and the beliefs you follow are a mix of your own and those of whatever people have arbitrarily surrounded you.

Whatever messages you've heard or seen most frequently, especially messages that have been communicated to you since you were young, are the "truths" that your subconscious will draw from to direct you down specific paths in your life. You can logically understand that a belief doesn't make sense and still be governed by it because something deep in your core tells you that it's real.

We can come to believe anything about ourselves through repetition. If you're continuously told, either through words or action, that you don't matter as much as other people, that you aren't special, or that you have no inherent value in this world, your brain will eventually regard these beliefs as factual knowledge.

Pavlov's dogs are a perfect example of how false and unhelpful information can be learned through repetition. In his most famous experiment, a study on classical conditioning, he consistently rang a bell just before feeding the dogs he studied. These dogs learned to associate the bell with food and started to drool and show other signs of excitement in response to hearing the bell before they could even see the food. They learned something that had no actual truth outside of the setting in which it was taught to them because of repeated exposure. There's no real connection between a bell and dog food.

When these dogs eventually left the laboratory, they continued to react to the sound of a bell as a precursor to being fed. Their brains considered the association between the bell and the dog food to be factual because for much of their lives, it WAS factual. The pairing happened so frequently that they didn't question the link, even though the link made no logical sense (and also because they were dogs.)

What are your bells? What did your childhood experiences teach you about the world in general that may not be universally true? That crying pushes people away? That anger is never appropriate? That nobody cares about your feelings? If you live your life under rules such as these, you've been conditioned to believe something false, and it's hurting you.

Essentially, we're all researchers who are studying ourselves. Unfortunately, we're both Pavlov and the dogs, which is an awful idea. Playing both roles, you will actively seek out and prioritize information that supports what you already believe. People don't change their minds easily about ideas they consider factual. That's why it's so rare for an adult to change religious or political beliefs. We interpret whatever we're presented with from the perspective we already have about what we believe to be true and correct. That perspective is entirely subjective and dictated by what we've been exposed to and conditioned to expect.

Beliefs we were exposed to in early childhood tend to be particularly "sticky" because young children cannot think critically. Their brains aren't structurally and developmentally ready to question what an adult tells them. They can't differentiate between a reasonable idea and an absurd idea. That's how my uncle once convinced me that he could open a beer bottle with his butt. I wasn't able to ponder the physics of the idea he was proposing, so I assumed it was a legitimate claim. To this day, a part of me still kind of believes he could do it. Children soak up everything around them, even if what's around them is poison.

Children also learn from how people treat them. We learn through repetition of experience just as much as through repetition of words. If people treat your fear, anger, or tears as annoyances or unimportant, you will "learn" that your feelings don't matter. Nobody has to say this to you directly for you to learn it. You'll believe that this is true of everyone in the world, that nobody cares about your feelings, even though it was only a few people who showed you this "truth."

If a need is not consistently met or is consistently unmet, young people usually can't just find someone else to meet it. Kids cannot choose new families, teachers, or neighbors. If you had unmet needs during your childhood, your only real option was to learn to ignore the need. The pain of feeling that unmet need became too intense to tolerate, so you tried to convince yourself you didn't need whatever it was that you were missing. You practiced tuning out from the part of yourself that needed reassurance, validation, or physical affection because it wasn't available to you. You built a dam around that part of your heart, and you stopped letting anything in or out. The dam doesn't just go away once you leave home. You can live your whole life with an unmet need and the means to meet that need right in front of you.

What if you learn that you don't matter as much as other people? What if you learn that healthy relationships are a myth? What if you learn that nobody follows their dreams? What if you learn that without money and prestige, you have no value as a person? These aren't truths; they're flawed perspectives with countless contradictory examples. But if your mind already regards them as accurate, you might miss these examples. These beliefs can dictate your entire life because they feel right to you, and you don't question them.

You would need hundreds, if not thousands, of new pieces of information to change your mind about something you've learned in childhood. No matter how long you live, you'll never gather enough information from outside sources to challenge a constantly running internal thought process. Even if you had millions of followers showering you with compliments on social media, you still only have access to them for a limited amount of time each day. Meanwhile, you're in dialogue with yourself nearly every waking second of your life. The most consistent voice you hear will always be yours.

So how do you unlearn unhelpful rules or beliefs? You don't, not exactly anyway. There's no way to just remove those formative experiences or statements from your mind. Fortunately, you don't need to. Just like you don't need to unlearn English to learn Spanish, you don't need to unlearn harmful beliefs to learn and live by new rules that better serve you. You just have to practice the new rules you want to live by, through both words and action, with such frequency that they override the previous set of rules.

The process of changing how you think is almost exactly like learning a new language. I speak, think, and write in English, and almost everything I hear is in English. It would be relatively easy for me to learn a few Spanish words, but those few words would never become a part of my natural thought process. It would require conscious effort for me to think of them and use them.

If I wanted to change my native language, to learn to think in Spanish instead of English rather than having to mentally translate my words before speaking, I couldn't just take a weekly class or practice for an hour or two a day. As long as most of what I hear, read, and write is in English, English will remain my native thought language. The only way I could learn to think in Spanish would be to immerse myself in that language so that Spanish was most or all of what I heard.

Currently, your mind is fluent in shame, doubt, insecurity, self-destruction, and hopelessness. We aren't trying to change a few conscious words here and there; we're trying to change the linguistic structure of your subconscious. We need to adjust the words you hear before they even reach your awareness so that you don't have to battle them constantly. I want you to immerse yourself in the language of your needs mattering. I want you to immerse yourself in the language of you belonging here, of you having and deserving a place in this world. If this life has taught you that you're somehow lesser than others, that you don't deserve happiness, or that you are fundamentally flawed in some way, then this life has taught you wrong.

Some of the repetition that you'll need for learning your new language is built into this book. You'll notice some points restated, some concepts revisited from different angles during our time together. That's intentional, and it's part of how I help people challenge unhelpful patterns. Therapy sessions involve a fair amount of repetition and re-statements because hearing something just once doesn't usually change anything. Someone with an average learning speed needs to hear or read a concept three times, with at least ten minutes spaced between each exposure, to commit that concept to memory. I can prime some of this learning for you, but this book by itself won't be enough. Not even close.

The messages you hear during your day need to change. Get out of your self-hatred echo chamber and start conducting some new research with an open mind. Actively seek out anything that reinforces what you want to feel and believe and decrease your exposure to anything that supports old, unhelpful belief systems. Surround yourself with people who tell you that you're enough. Only follow social media that builds you up rather than that which tears you down. Sell any books, music, or movies that reinforce old beliefs. Minimize your contact and interactions with people who keep you thinking the way you have been, to whatever extent you can. That's the only way to change this narrative and to unlearn the untrue.

Remember This:

How true something feels is a measurement of how frequently that belief or concept has been repeated to you, not a measurement of how real or accurate it is. Challenging these unhelpful beliefs requires frequent exposure to new, contradictory beliefs, and most of that will have to come from you. When you notice that you're stuck in old negative beliefs patterns like "I'm a failure" or "nobody cares about me," remind yourself of something like this:

"It only feels true because I keep hearing it."

HOPELESS

Someone told me that I'm hopeless today.
Someone who knows me very well.
He said it seems like I'm constantly searching for something.
But that I have no idea what it is.
And I wouldn't even know it if I found it.
He called it a "pointless, endless journey."
It felt a little awful to hear those things.
But it also felt amazing.
I had never felt so understood.
I didn't think anyone could see it.
But some of the other things he said scared me.
He said something "has me," and it isn't "letting go."
It's terrifying how accurate that feels.
I feel like there's a giant magnet underneath the earth.
Pulling things out of me.
I don't know how to stop it.
I want to dig until I find it.
I'll use whatever it takes.
I need to find it and destroy it.
I'll rip it apart.
Nothing will be OK until I do.
I want to feel again.
I want to hope again.
I have to stop this.

LIE #5: YOU'RE NOT TRYING HARD ENOUGH

For so many people, every morning starts with an overwhelming mental to-do list. You feel overloaded with stress before you even get out of bed. You work as hard as you can, only stopping to take breaks when you're feeling so drained that you aren't accomplishing anything. Your breaks are mostly periods of zoning out, scrolling, or staring at the television. You achieve some of your daily goals, but not as many as you wanted to. You don't feel much better, so you have a few beers or do a little online shopping to try and relax. You feel better for a little bit, followed by guilt or regret about "screwing up." The day is a loss. You go to bed stressing that you need to be better tomorrow.

Meanwhile, other people seem to just effortlessly accomplish things that are a constant internal struggle for you. They go to the gym, go to work, make healthy dinners, keep their house clean, and maintain a healthy and active social life with minimal visible stress or strain. They seem to just glide through life most of the time, not appearing to fight the internal war that dominates most of your days.

These people probably don't have any particular abilities that you lack. I doubt that they inherently have more energy or drive. They aren't necessarily any more intelligent or more ambitious than you. For the most part, they're people who have uncovered perhaps the biggest lie that our society self-perpetuates; the lie that we need to be under constant stress to get anything done.

The majority of us live under a chronically dysfunctional amount of pressure from simply managing our daily affairs. The complexity and expectations of modern society are unprecedented and almost incomprehensible. Most days feel like a marathon just to get to the end. We will do or take almost anything that makes us feel better in the moment, even if we know it'll be just another thing to worry about in the long run. Most of our stress comes from within. We set arbitrary goals and make pointless social comparisons to find ways we aren't "measuring up."

I want you to know that you don't have to do this. There is no basis for any of these comparisons. We differ so much from one person to the next, both in who we are and what we experience, that making a meaningful comparison between two people is a scientific impossibility. The number of inconsistent variables between you and whatever random person you decide you're supposed to measure up to is incalculable. You cannot accurately compare people. Even identical twins develop different personality traits, preferences, and lifestyles, each shaped by their unique experiences.

Our default reactions to feeling like we aren't doing good enough are maladaptive. We crank up the pressure internally. We criticize ourselves. We negatively compare ourselves to others. We remind ourselves of all the good things that will happen if we can just be more productive and all the bad things that will occur if we can't be. We judge our output without context as if we have no idea how stressful our own lives are. We make things worse.

There *is* a relationship between pressure and productivity, but it isn't linear. It's curvilinear, meaning that both too little pressure and too much pressure weigh us down. A moderate amount is what we need; we need to care about something and believe it's worth doing, but if it feels like a matter of life or death, we shut down. Where do you think you fall on this curve? Do you legitimately believe that you are struggling right now because you don't have enough stress?

You will naturally do your best work when you feel like your best self. The idea that we need to feel bad about ourselves to change or be productive is so backward it's ridiculous. We need to feel GOOD about ourselves to do our best work. That's a neurological truth shared by all mammals. The pull to move towards something positive is stronger than the pull to move away from something negative. We recognize this in other animals; dog training, for example, is based much more on reward than on punishment. Yet when we try to "train" ourselves to change our daily habits or routines, it's just punishment followed by more punishment.

I want you to consider giving up on this strategy. Give up on continually pushing yourself to be better. Give up on endlessly focusing on the "next" thing. Give up on living with your neck on a guillotine that could fall on any day you don't live up to arbitrary expectations. I know it seems like giving up will cause a backslide. It feels like if you ease off, even just a little, you'll accomplish even less. I know you're worried about "falling behind." You won't.

You need the exact opposite of what you've been giving yourself. Every time you feel pressure, respond internally with peace. Every time you feel the urgency, respond internally with patience. When you expect perfection from yourself, instead, try to expect completion. When you catch yourself thinking, "I'm worthless/lazy/stupid if I can't do this," respond with, "Whatever happens with this doesn't define me." Do these things not to soothe your feelings or to gratify yourself, but to put yourself in a mental place where you can accomplish more.

A good chef sharpens their knife before each use. They do

this for a pair of reasons. Naturally, the blade dulls a little bit each time it's used, and keeping a knife sharp helps it cut better. If you never sharpen a knife, it will lose its edge and no longer cut food effectively. The less apparent reason to keep it sharp is that working with dull knives is extremely dangerous. You have to press much harder on a dull knife to cut food, making it more likely that the blade will slip and more likely that you will significantly injure yourself if it does slip.

You are no different than that knife. Everything you do, in one way or another, wears you down. Over time, you lose your edge if you don't do the things that keep you sharp. Rest. Play. Connection. Nourishment. Purpose. You have to press harder and harder on yourself to get anything done. Years and years of slicing with minimal sharpening leaves you feeling like a butter knife trying to cut a potato. And just like a chef's knife, working when your edge has been dulled is dangerous. You're more accident-prone. More likely to cause damage to yourself or someone else.

There is no race. It's all an illusion. Whatever you've accomplished, whatever you have, whatever you do, there's no way to compare it to another person's versions of those things. The comparisons that social norms force us into are artificial and superficial. What does it matter how your grades compare to someone else's grades? Whether you are more or less athletic than they are? Who has more friends? People tell us early and often in our lives that these are proper measurement tools for determining a person's worth. They don't go away when we reach adulthood; they just change form. Salaries. Promotions. Houses. Cars. Our children's accomplishments.

None of it matters. You aren't running on a track, neck-and-neck with your competitors; you're carving an uncharted path through a dense forest. A path that's never been traveled before you came along. Your brain is different. Your body is different. Your childhood was different. Trying to get "ahead" in life is a fallacy. There is no ahead. There is no behind. There is just you and wherever you happen to be. That's it.

There is no great competition. There are moments of competition. Sometimes multiple people want the same job, or the same house, or the same partner. You'll win some of these competitions, and you'll lose some of them. So will everyone else. It doesn't mean anything. It's not part of a bigger narrative. We are not at war with one another. We are at war with ourselves.

No more living under the gun. No more chasing an idealized version of yourself. Starting today, we go forward at a measured, sustainable pace. We focus more on self-care than on arbitrary accomplishments. We don't just move the goalposts; we tear them down and walk away. You'll find productivity when you find peace.

Remember This:

Life can feel like a race, a competition against others. It isn't. There's no meaningful way to compare one person to another. Your journey is unique, your timelines for achieving your goals arbitrary. When you find yourself feeling insecure, inadequate, or that you are "behind" in some way, remind yourself of something like this:

"Nobody has traveled my path before."

HOPELESS PART 2

You're right about the magnet.
You're wrong about the location.
The magnet is inside of you.
You can't dig it out and rip it apart.
It isn't tangible.
The magnet is made out of your thoughts.
Your self-loathing.
So loud that it echoes inside.
Your perception of your isolation.
The way you exacerbate your alienation.
You ARE different.
But not nearly as much as you believe.
When you indulge your feelings of separation.
You further divide yourself from others.
You are human, and you do exist.
I know you have mixed feelings about that.
Slowly, you'll make peace with it.
You won't loathe your humanity indefinitely.
This is a journey of coming to terms with dualities.
In some ways, you are entirely alone.
In others, you are just like everyone else.

LIE #6: YOU AREN'T READY

Your mind has an override switch called the amygdala. It's fully formed at birth and doesn't change or evolve beyond that point. It's an emergency device that activates when it believes you're in danger. It wrestles control away from your conscious mind and temporarily transforms you into a more instinctual, reactive creature; a simpler mammal. It's scanning for danger constantly, even during the calm, quiet moments of your life.

The amygdala doesn't appear to have changed significantly in the hundreds of thousands of years humans have been on earth. That's in extreme contrast to our lifestyles and social structures, both of which have changed immensely throughout human history, particularly within the last 200 years or so. Many of us no longer face frequent threats to our physical safety and integrity. We don't often have to hunt each day to secure food. We usually don't need someone from our tribe to stand guard at night to watch for invaders. We aren't likely to die from a superficial wound becoming infected.

Our amygdalae (that's the plural for amygdala – I know it looks weird but just trust me) don't know this. They aren't designed for the generally safe but superficially stressful lifestyles that most of us have today. They continue to assess everything that happens to us in a day as if we're one misstep away from making a fatal mistake, which causes us to have a lot of "false alarms."

We're like the first generation of fish that emerged from the sea, walking on land and breathing air but trying to figure out why we still have gills. Our brains have some serious incompatibilities with our lifestyles. Creating a meaningful life beyond daily survival, pursuing goals like fulfillment, purpose, belonging, and love is something we're still learning how to do. These are "new" needs, and we haven't figured out how to meet them consistently. Knowing when your brain gets hijacked by ancestral concerns is essential if you want to have any shot of getting what you want from this life.

You don't attend to thoughts based on how realistic or important they are. You attend to thoughts based on how scary they are. The more threatening the idea, the more attention it gets, no matter how unlikely or far-fetched that thought might be. That's why the news and the weird clickbait banners on most websites are almost exclusively frightening or potentially disturbing stories. They scare you into viewing their advertisements or visiting their sites, profiting off of your fear by promising to show you the current reason you should be in a state of panic. Your amygdala is drawn to these fear-oriented stimuli. It needs to know what you might be up against, what tragedy might be lurking around the corner so that it can anticipate it and hopefully prevent it.

You know that sharp jolt of nervousness, fear, or anxiety you experience when you consider doing something unfamiliar? That voice that says, "don't try that, what if you mess up?" The invisible tape that appears over your mouth when you consider expressing a dissenting opinion in a group? That's your amygdala. Holding you back. Keeping you meek. Telling you that what you want is too much, not worth going after.

You're a risk-aversive creature because you've evolved to prioritize fear over other feelings. Fear registers on a much deeper level for you than opportunity, hope, excitement, or discontentment, and it has the last word in most of the choices you make. Back in our hunter/gatherer times, the anxious, cautious people lived the longest and produced the most offspring. When most days held the possibility of life-threatening danger, it was much wiser to assume an unidentified dark shape on the ground was a venomous snake and avoid it than it was to think it was a stick and pick it up. Most of our bold, brave, fearless ancestors died young because they didn't have enough fear to stay alive. Virtually everyone living today comes from a proud lineage of fearful, self-doubting, pessimistic worst-case thinkers because that was what they had to be to survive.

Your life is dramatically different than the lives of your distant ancestors, but your internal safety system is almost exactly the same as theirs. Decisions like what to major in, where to send our kids to school, and who to date or marry are the modern equivalent of deciding whether to travel hundreds of miles on foot over dangerous terrain or stay put and try to withstand a harsh winter. Everything still feels like a life-or-death decision, so your mind tells you not to do anything that holds even a slight chance of not working out. It's hard to want to take risks when the consequence of failure feels like literal death.

If you genuinely want more out of your life than sustained survival, if you're after consistent feelings of pride, accomplishment, belonging, and contentment, you're going to have to act contrary to what feels normal and natural. You'll have to disrupt your internal systems and start to reorganize them. You'll have to defy your mind because it isn't serving you the way you need it to. It doesn't want you to have joy or excitement nearly as bad as it wants you to have repetition and sameness. You can have the things you want from this life, but you're going to have to wade through a lot of fear to get there because your mind will fight you at every turn. It makes you afraid of success, fearful of dreams. It's stuck in the past, in more ways than one.

You can't trust your mind to lead you to happiness. You can trust it to direct you towards familiarity, which is often the antithesis of happiness. If you follow your impulses and intuitions, you generally travel in a loop. You go on a little journey that ends right where it began. As far as your limbic system is concerned, as long as you're still alive all is well. Making any change to the way you live will inherently feel threatening. Continuing to do what you instinctually feel like doing will keep you exactly the same person you currently are, living the exact same life you now are. Safe and under-stimulated in your homeostatic holding pattern.

Even if you aren't exactly happy with your life as it is today, you're used to it and you generally know what each day will bring. You're acclimated to dealing with feelings like frustration and disappointment, and they don't sting like they used to. You've become accustomed to your struggles and somewhat complacent in dealing with them. Coping with these feelings and challenges is still unpleasant, but it's no longer scary. It's just your daily life. Change is what scares you. Hope scares you. Newness scares you. The idea that you might try to make more out of your life than it is today but not succeed at it scares you.

We often want to feel "ready" before trying to make changes in our lives. That's why we don't usually change. Readiness is a trap, a convenient and believable excuse to stay stuck in pre-existing patterns. Neurologically speaking, a feeling of being ready to do something is a stamp of approval from your amygdala. When you wait to feel ready for something, you're waiting on the most conservative, pessimistic, anxious, worst-case-scenario part of your brain to assess your proposal and say, "everything is in order here."

Your amygdala will rarely approve of you wanting to do anything you haven't done at least a few times before. That's why feeling ready to do something and being ready to do something are two very different things. Your mind uses the past to predict the future. It tends to have overly pessimistic projections about doing anything that it doesn't have data on. That's why new people, challenges, and experiences always carry that sense of potential threat; they're unknowns, and therefore unpredictable. Your amygdala doesn't like unpredictable, so it steers you away from unknowns.

Your brain also doesn't understand who you are at this moment. The version of yourself that you see in your mind is almost certainly a bit outdated. First impressions are very, very hard to shake, and your first impressions of yourself are probably pretty unflattering. You remember being a child, mostly helpless and dependent upon everyone around you. You remember being dumped, getting fired, or failing a test. You remember every misstep, every social mistake, every embarrassment, every time you tripped and fell flat on your face.

Your mind counts all this against you, even today. Even if it was 40 years ago. Even if you're married and have kids, even if you have a million dollars in the bank, even if you have a doctorate (ask me how I know that one), your mind will never allow you to forget the running tally of everything you've ever screwed up. It files this information away and saves it strategically. When you ask yourself questions like "Can I really do this?" your mind will help you recall every memory of falling short to discourage you from trying something new and to help keep you in your safe little bubble. Right where it wants you to be.

That's why I want you to work on taking action before you feel ready. I want you to know and begin to trust that you're always at least one step beyond where you feel like you are. Your mind will need proof of what I'm saying. It won't just take me at my word, especially when those words contradict a script that's been running through your mind for your entire life. That proof can only come from taking action before you feel ready.

I'm comfortable sharing with you that I've never felt ready for anything I've done in my life that was even moderately important. I didn't feel ready to be a husband or a father, didn't feel ready for college or graduate school, and didn't feel ready to be a psychologist upon completing graduate school. At this very moment, I don't feel ready to be writing this book. The idea of it being released and read by other people legitimately terrifies me. Or, more accurately, it terrifies my amygdala.

I'm doing it anyway because of something I've learned along the way; most of the time, the feeling of being ready to do something comes a little bit after you start doing it. I've felt like I'd probably fail every step of the way on my journey. My fearful, risk-aversive mind told me I should quit my pursuits while I was ahead and work on trying to be satisfied with a life that was less than what I aspired to have. I heard it. I felt it. I just never listened. My parents will happily tell you I've never been a great listener. It's one of those "double-edged sword" types of situations.

You'll miss out on so many amazing things in your life if you wait to feel ready for them. Your mind just isn't very accurate at determining what you're truly capable of at the present moment. It assesses situations as being more dangerous than they are and causes you to be highly risk-aversive because it still thinks you're facing mortal danger every day of your life. It sees you as less capable and less resilient than you genuinely are today because it can't let go of who you used to be. You can start to live beyond the unrealistic limitations imposed upon you by your mind. Try to trust that you are a little bit beyond where you think you are and that almost nothing is as scary as it feels. Try to live your life from that place, and you might be amazed by what happens.

Remember This:

We're highly evolved to pay more attention to potential adverse outcomes than potential positive outcomes. We're unrealistically pessimistic about our future and ourselves. We unconsciously prioritize consistency over opportunity, routine over joy, and sameness over excitement. When you find yourself afraid to take on a new challenge, hesitant to walk a new path, or feeling like you won't be able to succeed

at something, remind yourself of something like this:

"Most of my fear and anxiety is an outdated survival response."

EMPTY

I go to where the people are.
But everything still feels empty.
I see people everywhere.
But I don't feel their presence.
Everything is cold.
The sound echoes.
The lights flicker.
Is there nothing here for me?
Where should I go?
Is there another world I can find?
That doesn't feel like this?
I have my little escapes.
My games.
My shows.
My books.
But the relief is so short-lived.
I need something that lasts.
I need a home.
I need my people.
I feel like there's a place out there for me.
Somewhere I'm supposed to be.
But I'm not there.
And I don't know how to find it.
Sometimes I'm afraid of my own mind.
I don't think anyone ever taught me how to use it.
How do I make it through this part?
I don't think I can take much more.

PART III: CHAINSAWS

"You're already the resident of your psychological domain; shouldn't you be the architect of it too?"

CARVE A NEW PATH

We're often told to control our thoughts and feelings, to be the "bigger person" in every situation. We aren't often told how we're expected to do this or what being in control of ourselves even means. What most would describe as "control," refusing to acknowledge your unpleasant or unwanted feelings and trying not to listen to your frequently negative internal narrative, is nothing more than simple repression. A basic and ultimately ineffective self-management technique.

Complete and total self-control isn't possible. There's just no getting around the fact that we're mammals. We have built-in overrides that take over the controls from us when we're exhausted, malnourished, or overwhelmed by stress. It's a neurological impossibility to be in complete control of yourself 24/7.

The internal structure of your mind is similar to a dense forest. When you're walking in the woods, you can theoretically travel in any direction at any time, but some pathways offer quite a bit more resistance than others. If there's already a path through the forest, you'll walk on that path automatically without thinking about it. Our minds typically choose the path of least resistance when left to their own devices. You won't often find yourself mindlessly wandering from the path to explore the uncharted parts of the forest. If you want to go there, you'll have to do it on purpose.

Your thoughts work the same way. There are "paths" in your mind, just like there are paths through the forest. When you've repeatedly had a series of ideas in sequence or simultaneously, they form a pathway. If I sing the first verse of a song you've heard a thousand times, you might sing the second verse without even thinking about it. That's a path. If your server at a restaurant says "enjoy your meal" and you respond with "you too," that's a path. If you think to yourself, "I'm such an idiot for telling my server to enjoy their food," that's a path.

The more frequently you travel these pathways, the more well-worn they become and the more likely you are to travel them again. The neurons that fire together wire together. Associations strengthen over time until they feel factual, unquestionable. It becomes harder and harder to see things any other way. You avoid the vines, thorns, and undergrowth of the unfamiliar and walk the same trail you walked last time.

I think control is being able to decide when you want to walk the paths that are already worn down for you and when you want to stray from the path and go a different way. It's being able to eventually wear down a new path so that you travel it naturally, without having to force yourself to do it. It's allowing the old and unhelpful paths to decay, letting them grow over with brush, weeds, plants, and trees so that you don't inadvertently continue to walk them even though you don't like the destinations they lead you to.

You're out there all alone, and it's a big, dark forest. What you're trying to do, to reject the path and create your own way through your own force of will, is amazing. Don't lose sight of that. Look at it with an overhead view, like you're an eagle soaring above it all. Picture that forest, dense and unyielding, stretching for miles in every direction. See all the people walking the premade path, trudging along without joy or excitement, resigned to their destination.

Branching out from the main path is a short, incomplete pathway. It isn't well worn. It looks rough, hastily carved. Where that new, unfinished path ends, you see a single human. They're exhausted, sweating, breathing heavily. You can see the determination in their eyes, the discontentment that brought them to this place. They've realized that the main path isn't for them, and they've come to understand that nobody who came before them has made a path that's quite right for them. They've decided to make their own. And they have a chainsaw.

The strategies in this section are your chainsaws. You can use them to carve out new pathways through your mind. You don't have to continue to think the way you've been thinking. Your mind belongs to you, and it should work for you. It should produce thoughts that benefit you, feelings that help you move forward and make healthy choices. It should recall relevant and useful memories instead of a constant anti-highlight reel of the worst things that have ever happened to you. It's fully capable of doing all of these things with some guidance from you.

You can use these strategies to carve whatever path you want. When branches and trees block your path, saw them down. When thorns grow on the new path, walk right through them and keep going. Eventually, the old path starts to become overgrown. When that happens, it turns cumbersome and uncomfortable to walk the path of self-loathing. It takes more effort to conjure up the negativity, bias, and pessimism that formed those pathways than it does to walk the new path you've created. A path of freedom from self-blame, powerlessness, emptiness, hollowness, and dissatisfaction with life.

I want to be clear; these aren't quick fixes. You're one person trying to cut your way through a forest. Progress will be slow. So slow you won't even see it every day. On your worst days you might feel like you're losing ground, like the trees are growing back faster than you can fell them. They aren't. Learn and practice these strategies, and there are only two ways you won't eventually get where you want to be; you either get impatient with yourself and try to rush things, or you become frustrated and give up. Please be patient with yourself. What you're trying to do is extremely difficult, but I know it's possible.

EMPTY PART 2

Nothing outside feels alive.
When you feel dead inside.
But you aren't dead.
Far from it.
You are simply dormant.
Like the brown grass hiding under a blanket of snow.
Hibernating through a harsh winter of life.
I promise you're still in there.
Intact as always.
Incubating in your shell.
Waiting for the right moment to emerge.
It won't happen all at once.
It will be slow, gradual.
You won't even notice when it begins.
The awareness will startle you.
When you look back on recent days and realize.
"I'm here again."
"Like I used to be."
Your only mission right now.
Is to survive this part.
That's it.
Just make it through to the next.
When everything starts to change.

SILENCE, CRITIC

The narrative is constant. Something nags at you, chips away at you, and criticizes your every move. It's the voice in your head, the one that sounds like your own but uses other people's words. The one that never forgets a mistake. The one that yanks excitement or joy from your grasp with a bombardment of worst-case scenarios. The one that over-interprets the words and the tones of your loved ones to sound harsh, critical, and shaming. It's the dark shadow that looms over every positive experience in your life. It's your critical inner monologue, a mortal enemy masquerading as a concerned friend.

We learn to be self-critical by internalizing judgments we hear and feel from other people. Nobody begins life with negative feelings toward themselves. We're taught these habits, learn these patterns. They're the messages that were repeated to us during our childhoods:

"You can always do better."

"Don't get too full of yourself."

"Calm down; you're too excited."

"Stop acting like you're special."

"Get over yourself."

"That's not good enough."

There can be a degree of truth and wisdom in statements like these, but they tend to become overgeneralized in our minds. Many of us first hear these phrases early in life, long before we have the ability to understand things like nuance and subtlety. We take them literally and apply them globally, whether that's how they were meant or not.

People aren't always careful with their words, and we get caught in the crossfire. Their statements echo in our minds, stealing our feelings of pride and accomplishment. These sayings become global rules we rigidly adhere to instead of situational pieces of guidance. Their ideals become barricades that wall us off from living the life we want and from experiencing the feelings we crave.

If your critical narrative is your mortal enemy, why do you treat it like a trusted friend? Why do you take its words to heart, hanging on its every sentence like gospel? Why do you drop hobbies, pursuits, or relationships when it tells you to? Why do you still act like it has your best interests in mind when it's done nothing but hold you back?

Probably because it doesn't identify itself as an enemy. It's disguised as you. There's no internal differentiation between these harsh, judgmental thoughts you've absorbed from others and your natural internal narrative. As long as it looks like you, sounds like you, and uses your words, you're going to treat it like it has your back and wants to help you.

I propose that we remove this misleading disguise and assign it a new form. A form more fitting to its true nature.

I want you to think of someone you don't respect. Someone who naturally makes you want to argue with them even if they say something reasonable. Someone whose mannerisms, tone of voice, and general appearance provoke feelings of defiance and opposition within you. It can be anyone. It can be someone you know in your personal life. It can be a famous person, a politician, or a celebrity. It can even be a fictional character.

This individual is the new personification of your inner

critic. Every thought that holds you back, brings you down, or steals from you no longer belongs to you. It now belongs to them. It comes from them. I want you to practice hearing your critical narrative in their words. Take the exact statements, the same beliefs, the same criticisms you hear all day long in your mind and attribute them to this person instead of yourself. Imagine their mannerisms, their posture, their tone of voice. Imagine everything about them that makes you want to fight back against their words.

Let's say you assign your inner critic to the form of Gaston from Beauty and the Beast. When you identify that you're experiencing a self-critical thought, press pause on the process and imagine Gaston saying it to you in your mind. Picture his posture and body language, his facial expressions. Hear it is in his tone of voice, with his undeserved arrogance and his subtly hostile narcissism. When it's not you telling yourself you aren't good enough but him instead, doesn't it make you want to fight back?

Allow yourself to fight back. Unleash your torrent of words against them. Tell them why everything they say is wrong. Tell them how they know nothing about you. Do not hold back. Do this again and again. You can do it in your mind, or you can do it verbally. You can yell. You can scream. You can punch things, although I strongly prefer that they be nonliving.

I want you to win every argument you have with this person. Never let them have the last word again. Rip their ridiculous positions to shreds. Make them cry. Make them apologize. Make them beg for mercy, then deny it to them. Keep going. Send them back into the nonexistence they came from until only you are left standing. Take back your mind from the hostile invaders that have taken up residency there. Make it somewhere you once again enjoy inhabiting.

Remember This:

Imagine your critical internal narrative taking the voice of someone other than you, someone you don't respect, someone who naturally makes you want to defy and argue. Start talking back to your critical narrative, and make sure you get the last word in. Over time, this defiance changes how you see yourself. It builds a sense of confidence and esteem and makes you less afraid of the world.

REWRITE THE RESEARCH

You probably think you know things about yourself. Things like:

"I'm not very smart."

"I'm fat."

"I'm ugly."

"I'm a loser."

"I'm a failure."

"I'm not good enough."

"I'm unlovable."

"I'm a bad spouse/parent."

You don't know these things. They can't be known. They aren't factual descriptions of a person. They're dynamic, subjective appraisals. At best, you have a series of theories.

You hold theories about yourself, theories about other people, and theories about the world. Theories that you treat as fact because you have some measure of evidence to support them. People *have* rejected you. You *have* failed at some things. You haven't *always* done right by others. Some of these things may have happened frequently. None of them tell the whole story of your life.

Your mind likes to look for patterns, and it will happily create them out of nothing. It threads these unpleasant experiences together, convincing you that they represent some sort of meaningful pattern in your life. You align with this theory, identify with it. It dictates how you see things, how you interpret your life. Your belief in the validity of these patterns places blinders on your perception. It funnels you, keeps you on the path of believing in it. It tricks you into only seeing what it wants you to see.

When you believe in the pattern, every day of your life becomes a poorly conceptualized research project. You think you already know the answers, and you seek out data that confirms these answers. Inevitably, you find some. Not *everybody* likes you. You don't succeed at *every* endeavor. *Some* people say hurtful things to you. It's not that these experiences don't count or don't mean anything. It's that you disregard the experiences that don't fit what you consider to be "the pattern," even if there are more experiences that don't fit than experiences that do fit.

You've seen contradictory evidence for nearly every belief you hold about yourself. Everyone who believes themselves to be a failure has had success at something. Everyone who thinks they're ugly has been attractive to someone. You allow your theories to dictate your reality. They become the assumed story of your life. They persist, sometimes even growing stronger over time because we assume their validity and we never test them.

Let's start testing them.

Your mind will automatically search for information or experiences that it can manipulate into fitting "the pattern." It's doing that already, daily, without any assistance from you. What it won't do without your conscious direction is seek out information that breaks the mold. It won't attend to data that suggests your theory is wrong. It throws out anything that doesn't fit, considers it an outlier. It does so with statements like these:

"He doesn't really like me. He was just being nice."

"Just because I did well on that test doesn't mean I'm smart. It was probably a really easy test."

"The only reason they haven't fired me yet is because they're desperate for employees."

"She doesn't love me. She would leave me if someone better came along."

To gather accurate information about the validity of your theories, you need to stop acting like you already know the answer. You need to be willing to re-examine what you consider to be confirmed with an open, inquiring mind and consider all data equally relevant. The data you've collected so far is tainted. Unfairly influenced by outside sources.

When you identify a personal belief system that you want to test, work on adding the phrase "I have a theory that" to the beginning of the belief system. Use linguistic adjustments like these:

Instead of "I always screw things up," say, "I have a theory that I always screw things up."

Instead of "Nobody will ever love me," say, "I have a theory that nobody will ever love me."

I'm sure you get the point. Changing the language that you use to describe what you believe instantly changes your perception of that belief. You may even notice a slight shift while reading this. What you once considered an inarguable fact that dictated your life becomes a questionable, testable theory with nothing more than a simple wording tweak.

Now that you've reframed your belief as a theory, you need to put yourself in situations where the theory can potentially be proven wrong. Go out and live your life without assuming you're a worthless, universally hated screwup and pay very close attention to what happens. When you have an experience that contradicts one of your theories, try not to automatically discount that experience. Consider it valuable data, a piece of evidence that challenges what you once considered to be a universal truth.

The convenient thing about the black and white nature of belief systems is that even if your attempt to challenge the belief system is only a partial success, you'll still effectively challenge it. If you achieve anything, you aren't a failure. If even one person finds you lovable, you aren't unlovable. If you notice and attend to these experiences, they can open the door to an entirely new set of beliefs about yourself.

Remember This:

Consider your negative beliefs as theories, not facts. Think of each day as a research project, and try to pay attention to data that doesn't support or even contradicts your negative beliefs. Don't accept a one-sided version of your life story.

STILL ALIVE

Why do so many things die.

While I'm still alive.

I'm not even enjoying this.

I wouldn't even be mad.

I tried to test my mortality today.

We had a bridge to cross.

Below was rushing water. Rapids. Rocks.

Crossing the top of the bridge was the logical solution. The path my friends chose.

I decided to cross it from below.

To inch my way across the narrow beams.

Falling would have hurt. A lot.

I didn't care. I didn't care about much at all on this particular day.

The feelings that should have been there simply weren't.

Halfway across, I decided it was too easy.

"Throw some rocks at me!" I shouted to my friends below.

They weren't the type to protect me from my poor choices. They happily obliged.

As I crossed the beams under a hail of stones, I started to feel something. Just a little, but it was there.

I was a little afraid. A little excited. And I was having just a tiny bit of fun.

I noticed something else too.

The rocks didn't hurt.

I felt them land, but it wasn't pain.

It was more of an acknowledgment.

Like somebody knocking on a door.

But I didn't answer.

Decided not to let them in.

I'm starting to worry that I do that too often.

Don't answer the door, that is.

Nothing gets in anymore.

It's lonely.

I don't want to be like this anymore.

DON'T LET THEM IN

Sometimes, in the depths of your mind, you'll find things that don't belong to you. Impulses to engage in behaviors that run contrary to your character. Thoughts that are inconsistent with who you understand yourself to be. Feelings that don't match your perspective on a situation. Some of these may disturb you. You might worry that you're changing into something callous, cynical, dark, or angry.

I want you to know that all of these things are completely normal. We're all exposed to an overwhelming amount of information each day, and a lot of it is unpleasant. The news. Social media. Other people's feelings, opinions, and experiences. Some of it gets in. It impacts you, changes you. It makes you a little more like everyone else and a little less like you.

It's crucial to preserve yourself, to hold on to whatever distinguishes you from others. If you don't consciously monitor everything that wants to make its way inside you can eventually become a numerical mean, a statistical average of what it means to be human. You'll often feel pressure to override anything that makes you unique with something that makes you fit in, to sand off your "rough edges" that make you unlike other people.

There's no way to be unaffected by the realities of the imperfect world that we inhabit, but you can minimize how much you absorb. You can protect your mind, keep your internal experience as pristine and untouched as possible. You can designate your inner world as a national forest area that the world's logging machines are forced to cut around.

To do this, you need to delineate where you begin and where you end. You need to claim a small piece of this world as your private mental space. A space that follows you wherever you go, whatever you do, and keeps you safe and protected.

Visualize some sort of boundary or barrier encompassing you. It should be large enough to fit your entire self into it and allow you a comfortable amount of space within. It should also be translucent, so that you can see out of it and still perceive and experience the world. Basically, a giant bubble that can never be popped. Your bubble is always with you, keeping you safely contained within it. It is your precious, sacred space. It belongs only to you, and nobody can take it from you.

This bubble is a visual representation of your mental filter. Everything inside of the filter belongs to you. Your thoughts, your feelings, your beliefs, and your experiences reside within it. Your hobbies, interests, passions, and pursuits belong here. Everything important and relevant to you. You alone are responsible for the contents of your bubble. Only you can choose to allow ideas or beliefs to enter or exit your protected space.

Everything outside of the bubble belongs to the world. You aren't responsible for anything that doesn't belong to you. You aren't able to control anything outside of your space. You only need to control what is yours. You need to protect your space and prevent anything damaging or destructive from entering it. Harmful and destructive things will continue to exist. You don't need to prevent that. You cannot prevent that.

Your mental space follows the same rules as your physical space. Consider the rules of your room, your apartment, your home, your office, or whatever other parts of the physical world belong to you. The contents of that space are yours. You choose how to arrange them. You decide what to keep, what to discard, and what to add. The purpose of this space is to enrich your life, to be as functional as possible for your specific and unique needs. It is not for anybody else. Only you.

When someone shares an experience, an opinion, a thought, or a belief with you, they are offering you something. They are presenting you with something that belongs to them and asking if you would like them to share it with you. They won't always phrase such things as requests, but ultimately that's all they can be. You're the landlord of your private mental space. As an adult, you get to decide who and what can take up residency there and who has to find somewhere else to live. It isn't your responsibility to find a home for the things you choose not to take in. They don't belong to you.

You don't have to take what they offer. Sometimes you might want to, and that's fine. Sometimes you might not want to, and that's also fine. It's always your choice, even if other people act like it isn't.

Practice keeping what belongs to others outside of your mental filter until you've had a chance to evaluate what they're offering you and decide what you want to do with it. Treat the ideas, concerns, and perspectives of other people like family heirlooms that have been brought to your doorstep and offered to you. You aren't obligated to accept them. You may wish to accept them, and that's fine. Maybe they're significant to you. Perhaps they go well with what you already own. Or perhaps the family heirloom is something that disgusts you. Maybe it's an inexplicably creepy clown painting that you want as far away from your living space as possible. You don't have to let it in. All of your spaces, including your mental space, belong to you.

Remember This:

Work on mentally separating what belongs to you and should be a part of your life from what you've accidentally picked up along the way. Visualize your protective bubble to remember where your responsibility and ownership of things begins and ends. When you find something inside that doesn't

belong to you, try not to claim it or align with it. Maintain your mental space just as you would your physical space. Don't let anything in that doesn't benefit you in some way.

SEE WHAT NOBODY ELSE CAN SEE

Imagine a sporting event or a concert where the crowd didn't react to anything that happened. Picture the attendees watching the action in stoic silence, not moving or voicing any response to what they were seeing. Think of how unappreciated, unwanted, and invalidated the athletes who were competing or the artists who were performing would feel. The message would be silent but clear; nobody cares.

It would devastate them. We thrive on feeling appreciated, love experiencing positive reactions to our efforts, whether we're in the public eye or not. Cheers and praise motivate us to push ourselves further, to take that next step, to keep going. Yet this lifeless crowd, this feeling of performing for an empty auditorium, is exactly how many of us feel much of the time. We do what we're told to do, and most of the time we get no response, no reaction, no celebration.

Unfortunately, most of us will never be fully appreciated by the world. So many of our best efforts and our most significant victories are internal. Unless you have some incredibly supportive and understanding people in your life, nobody's going to celebrate your first shower after three days of laying in bed, debilitated by depression or grief. Nobody will cheer you on for eating breakfast when you have no appetite, no motivation, and no energy.

Nobody except you.

Your crowd, your audience, isn't the people you interact with. Your audience lives in your mind. You're the narrator of your own experience. Your feedback for yourself lands the hardest. It's powerful enough to drown out everything around you. The entire world could celebrate you, and you'd feel nothing if you weren't also celebrating yourself.

I learned this by accident when I was 19. I had recently moved out on my own, my second attempt at doing so after trying to live in a dorm for a year and generally failing at most everything. Things weren't going much better this time around. I was only going to class half the time, hated my job, was isolating myself, and was barely caring for myself or my apartment.

On some random day, I felt a tiny hint of motivation. One of those unexpected moments where things feel just a bit lighter for no particular reason. I decided to use this surprising burst of energy to vacuum, which I hadn't done in about a month. To my amusement, the thought, "Look at those straight lines! He's doing a great job picking up all that dirt!" popped into my head. I'd been watching a lot of football the previous day, one of the only things I still enjoyed at that time, and listening to the commentators all day had apparently impacted my thought process. Strange and cheesy as it was, it gave me a desire to keep working. I wanted more praise, even if only from my inner John Madden ghost.

That little moment changed my life, one of so many seemingly random and unpredictable turning points. I consciously kept that voice going all day. Hearing someone praise me for my efforts, even if it was only a voice in my head, made me want to work harder. It felt like I had a crowd, an audience that appreciated what would look insignificant to anyone other than me. By the end of the day, I'd deep cleaned my apartment, applied for three jobs, and bought a used exercise bike. I accomplished more on that day than in the previous month combined.

We all need an internal cheering section of some kind.

Feeling appreciated and celebrated is a universal human need, and the world won't always respond to us in a way that gives us these feelings. We always have the option to give them to ourselves.

Try narrating your day today from a different perspective than usual. Instead of the judgmental, critical, harsh narrator you're used to hearing, try to cultivate an inner voice that is genuinely excited about whatever you do. Be your own soccer announcer and scream yourself mentally hoarse describing the intricate details of a typical day. Celebrate every little action you take with that level of vigor, no matter how fake it feels at first.

Work on giving this gift to yourself. Develop and use this voice. Practice it, encourage it, and work on making it a natural response to every accomplishment you have, big or small.

It will feel awkward and unnatural. Push through that. It will feel silly and maybe even a little condescending. Push through that. If you're really struggling to identify the little victories, try this strategy; think of everything in your day that you would criticize yourself for if you didn't do it. Would you criticize yourself for not taking a shower? Not getting the mail? Not doing the dishes? If so, then doing those things must be a success. The options are success or failure, not failure or nothing. It's only logical. Reward yourself for everything you do that you would punish yourself for if you didn't do it.

Once you start to genuinely believe that every little thing you do right every single day counts for something, you won't be at the mercy of the world to give you the feedback you need to hear. Feedback that it's often frustratingly unwilling to distribute. Don't be invisible to yourself. Credit yourself for the victories that only you know about. Cheer yourself on when all seems bleak. Give yourself a home-field advantage in your own life.

Remember This:
Practice internally celebrating every victory, no matter how

minor. If it helps, picture an announcer or a crowd reacting to everything you do well in a day. Celebrate and reward yourself for the many things you do right that nobody but you can see.

STILL ALIVE PART 2

I know why you don't really feel pain anymore.
Why you know it's there, but it doesn't have the sting it once did.
It's because you've reached your threshold.
You're all scabbed and calloused inside.
Your nerve endings buried under scars.
Too deep down to register anything more than a dull ache.
They can't hurt you anymore.
They're welcome to try.
But there's not much left that they can do.
That hasn't already been done to you.
You see, I have a theory.
I think you've already survived the worst of it.
You took every shot, absorbed every blow.
And you're still here, still alive.
They tried to destroy you.
But they failed.
You retreated inside of yourself.
Built a bomb shelter and locked the door.
Now you sit, waiting.
Wondering if it's safe to emerge.
They've taught you that you can survive anything.
Because they've tried everything.
I want you to try something for me today.
Unlock that door and come out.
You'll see them right away.
Guns still pointed at you.
But I think they're out of ammunition.
And all you have to do to win is to keep walking forward.

To survive.
To live.
I wonder what they will think.
When you walk right past them.

HACK THE EQUATION

Motivation and willpower are scams. They exist, but most people don't understand how they work and massively overstate their importance. Not having enough of one or both of them is used to explain nearly every struggle, every failure, every unrealized dream. Didn't get the grade you wanted? Must not have been motivated! Stopped going to the gym? Not enough willpower! I always wondered; if hating myself and my life isn't enough motivation to change, what would be?

It was an unanswerable question because I was trying to understand a faulty explanation. Motivation isn't a precursor to success or action; it's an outcome of them. It's created mainly through the release of dopamine in your brain, which often happens after realizing an accomplishment or completing a task. In other words, motivation isn't there to help you get going; it's there to help you keep going. And if you aren't experiencing feeling of rewards because you're depressed or anxious or traumatized, you don't experience much motivation either.

Willpower can help you get started on something, but that's pretty much where its usefulness ends. It's a finite resource, and it's impossible to sustain anything indefinitely with willpower alone. No matter how badly you want something, if the only thing keeping you going is willpower, the behavior will stop as soon as your willpower runs out. And it will eventually run out. Do you think people who practice habits consistently for years on end are using willpower to do it every day? They aren't. They've hacked their decision making equation to make the change stick.

When you consider taking action, your mind assesses the proposition almost instantaneously. In most cases, you've already decided whether or not you'll do something before you even fully realize that you're considering it. You subconsciously weigh relevant variables and initiate the behavior or begin to resist the behavior immediately. If your initial response was a "no," it's tough to change your mind.

That's why you often feel tremendous internal resistance to things you genuinely want to do, or at least things you want to get done. That heavy, weighty feeling that comes over you when you consider getting up off the couch to do a load of laundry or put the dishes away. The reason your body suddenly seems to weigh 2,000 pounds when it's time to get out of bed and start preparing for work. The way your brain decides to stop thinking in words when you try to write a paper or compose an email. You aren't trying to make a choice; you're trying to override a choice that's already been made for you.

There's a workaround to this. A "hack" of sorts. To apply it, you have to understand how your internal motivation system works.

Whether you feel like doing something or not is determined by your perception of the effort it will take to accomplish that task in contrast with your perception of the reward you will experience when you complete the task. If you believe that the effort required to complete the task will be greater than the anticipated reward of completing the task, you generally won't complete the task (or even start the task) unless there's some external force pressuring you to do so. Most of what we want to get done in a given day falls under this category because of the immense pressure we all live under, and because of the lies we listen to that rob us of our ability to feel the full reward of our accomplishments.

If you believe that the effort required to complete the task will be roughly equivalent to the anticipated reward of completing the task, it's a toss-up. You might do it if you're bored or if the mood strikes you. It won't be something you can count on, but it won't necessarily be a battle either. It will just be one of those "sometimes" things.

If you believe that the effort required to complete the task will be less than the anticipated reward of completing the task, you'll naturally complete the task again and again without really needing to consider it. It's either so low-effort that you don't mind doing it or so high-reward that you want to keep doing it to experience the feeling that comes after. These are the behaviors that quickly become habits, the things you don't have to think about; you naturally gravitate towards them.

If you can change the variables in the equation so that you consider a task to be either lower effort or higher reward than you currently perceive it to be, it becomes easier to initiate that behavior. It also decreases your mental load, as it's one fewer decision to ruminate about during your day. You can just DO things, and your life won't feel quite so much like a war of attrition with yourself. It's like switching existence to easy mode.

Anything that makes a task easier to complete makes you more likely to do it. One consideration here is logistics. You want to make the tasks you're trying to engage in more often as accessible as possible. If you want to spend more time creating art, but your art supplies are buried at the bottom of a closet, you've created a scenario where starting an art project requires an awful lot of effort. If you want to start a fitness routine, but you've decided you have to work out with a personal trainer at a gym 20 minutes from home, you have to overcome a lot of barriers just to go work out. Try to remove as many logistical obstacles between yourself and the desired behavior as possible so that your mind assesses the activity more favorably.

You can also invert this process if you want to STOP doing something. If you have a goal of reducing mindless snacking, don't leave snacks in a location where you can mindlessly access them. If you want to drink a little less after work, don't store your beer in the kitchen fridge. Remember that every additional step you have to take to engage in a behavior, no matter how small, is an extra chain in the process and an additional chance for you to say "no."

Another way to decrease the perception of effort involved in a task is to lower your expectations. Perfectionism is a detriment to productivity because it makes everything you do seem that much harder. If you tell yourself that a task has to be completed flawlessly and you don't feel like you have the time or energy to complete that task flawlessly, you probably aren't going to even start it. Try shifting your expectations for yourself from "perfect" or even "excellent" to simply "complete." If that task legitimately needs to live up to some particular standard, you can build up to that standard once you're in the habit of engaging in the task.

There are also quite a few ways you can make a task more rewarding to complete. One is to take a brief moment of mindfulness upon completing the task to ensure your brain registers that it's complete and that you did a good job. It isn't so much the completion of a task as it is your acknowledgment of completing a task that produces feelings of reward. That feeling doesn't come automatically, and you can miss it entirely if your day is just one task after another. That's why sometimes you can have an extremely productive day and logically understand that you accomplished a lot but still feel like you did nothing.

Look at your closet or your drawers after you put your laundry away and observe how nice and organized they are. Take a moment to admire your lawn after a good mow. These moments stimulate your reward pathways, giving you a dopamine hit that makes you want to engage in the behavior again. When you refuse to reward yourself for your accomplishments you weaken your reward pathway for that behavior, decreasing your motivation to do it again.

It can also help to set process goals instead of outcome goals. Outcome goals are what you hope will happen in response to your efforts. Wanting to get 8 hours of sleep is an outcome goal. Wanting to save $1,000 is an outcome goal. Wanting to lose 10 pounds is an outcome goal. The problem with outcome goals is that these outcomes aren't entirely within your control. Whether they happen or not is determined by a combination of your actions and random life events. If you set the goal to get 8 hours of sleep and you go to bed on time, but a child or a pet or an ambulance wakes you up in the middle of the night and you have trouble falling back asleep, you've failed at your goal. This isn't fair, because you did everything you were supposed to.

Process goals focus exclusively on your contributions to the outcomes and prevent you from taking false responsibility for chance events. In the above example, a process goal would be "be in bed by 10:00 pm." Whatever happens from there isn't on you. You did what you needed to do. You met your goal, and that will give you at least a slight sense of reward no matter what else happens.

One particularly effective strategy to simultaneously decrease the perception of effort and increase the perception of reward is to start small in your endeavors. When you're trying to initiate a new behavioral habit such as being physically active, eating healthier, getting more sleep, or being more social, don't expect yourself to be able to flip a switch overnight and be dramatically different tomorrow than you are today. Human beings don't work that way.

Begin with the smallest increment possible in whatever it is that you're trying to do. Work out for five minutes. Make one food substitution. Go to bed ten minutes earlier. Text one friend. Give yourself a goal you can efficiently complete again and again so that you set yourself up to succeed. Use all of these strategies to trick your brain into doing what you want it to do more often.

Remember This:

Don't try to change your habits through motivation or willpower. Focus on modifying your perceptions of reward and effort through making changes like decreasing perfectionistic expectations, removing logistical barriers, mindfully appreciating your efforts, and making small changes instead of large ones. Build your momentum gradually and trust in yourself instead of micromanaging yourself. Always give yourself credit for the things you do so that you want to do them again.

LOOK BEYOND YOUR LIMITS

There are a lot of arbitrary limits in life. Most cars come with electronic top-speed governors to prevent you from pushing the vehicle to its limits. Most computer processors have software limitations keeping them from reaching their maximum clock speed and potentially overheating. Some people love to override these limits and push their devices to their maximum possible state of functioning.

You have an arbitrary limit too. An artificial barrier inside of you that won't let you push beyond a certain point. An archaic failsafe attempting to protect you from disappointment and failure by keeping you out of situations where there's a nonzero chance of a letdown. You've felt it before. You consider taking a risk or pushing yourself beyond your comfort zone in some way. Maybe you're thinking about going back to school for an advanced degree or applying for a job that's significantly beyond your current position in stature and compensation. As you're thinking about taking your first step, you feel like someone slammed on the brakes. Your motivation and drive come to a halt, and you decide you should just be happy with what you have.

That feeling, that moment when your dreams die, is your arbitrary limit hard at work.

Want to know how to override it?

It exists because you have no way to accurately predict

who you'll be in the future. You know that you'll continue to learn and grow to some extent, but there's no way to be certain of exactly what these changes will look like. When you visualize something you might do in a month, a year, or even five years, you don't know exactly who you'll be when that time comes. Future you is a mystery, a wildcard, a total unknown. Since your mind can't know precisely who future you is, it substitutes what it considers to be the closest approximation; present you.

This is where you hit your arbitrary limit. Your mind has a hard time allowing you to plan for or commit to something in the future that present you might not be capable of doing. It slams on the brakes, cuts off your resources, and drains your motivation to prevent you from going "too fast.". As a result, you always live a step or two behind your capability. You continuously underestimate yourself and sell yourself short because your concept of yourself lags behind your actual capabilities.

If you want to work around this processing error, you need to consciously see your future differently. Imprint this concept into your mind and don't let it go; future you and present you are not the same. You'll have time to become the person you will need to eventually be along the way to your destination. As you work towards accomplishing your long-term life goals, you will slowly evolve into a person capable of living them out. Try to trust in this. Work on believing in your ability to learn, to grow, to adapt. Try to "look beyond" the limitations of your current persona.

I know it's kind of a lofty concept, but you're my living proof that it's real. Aren't you doing things regularly today that would have completely overwhelmed you a few years ago? I'm confident that, without even looking very hard, you can find at least one significant part of your current life that would have been met with a hard "no" in your relatively recent past. Yet here you are, doing it, and generally doing it well.

Never assume your limitations. Always assume that you'll continue to grow, learn, and evolve and that future you is more capable and more resilient than present you. Assume that your experiences in our imperfect world have artificially and negatively impacted your self-concept and self-image. Assume that you've fallen victim to cultural norms emphasizing self-deprecation and the celebration of failure.

Don't allow the course of your life to be dictated by your status at any particular arbitrary moment in time. You're a dynamic being, a creature in a constant state of evolution. You'll surprise yourself again and again with just how capable and resilient you are, as long as you put yourself in situations where you have the opportunity to develop and grow these traits.

In other words, assume that you are so much more than you assume. And act accordingly.

Remember This:
Don't project an unchanged version of yourself into the future and assume struggles or failure. Instead, try assuming that you will learn and grow in the ways that you need to between now and then. Practice trusting your ability to adapt and evolve as necessary to take on challenges that currently seem overwhelming to you.

TWO PEOPLE

Where did I go?
I was here once.
I used to hunt for frogs.
I used to swim in the river.
I used to care about what happened to my body.
Life felt like an adventure.
Was that even real?
Those moments are so far away now they feel like I dreamt them.
Fabricated.
Intangible.
Impossible.
Are these even my memories?
Or did someone else put them there somehow?
Maybe they're imprinted, like the replicants from Blade Runner.
It doesn't seem like that could have ever been me.
Nothing's the same anymore.
How was I so carefree?
I feel like two people living in one body.
But only one of them feels real.
I think the other one died.

ASK THE RIGHT QUESTIONS

I totally understand the pull to find the answers. I know how much the questions can burn inside.

"Why am I the way I am?"

"Why did that have to happen to me?"

"Where did this all go so very wrong?"

"Could things have been different for me?"

It's understandable to want answers to these questions. But it's a waste of time and energy to search for them.

You'll probably never find an answer that fully satisfies you. For many of us, there is no singular sentinel event that dramatically altered the course of our lives and set us upon our current path. Our present struggles are more often caused by an accumulation of adverse events throughout our lives interacting in an incalculably complicated manner to produce our everyday experience. The world's most advanced supercomputer couldn't untangle that web. It's beyond human comprehension.

Some of our lives were changed in an instant, our safety shattered by a defining traumatic event. Even then, the various ways that those around us handled the fallout of that event often has a much more significant impact on how that event changes us than the event itself. Trauma isn't always devastating when we receive support, validation, understanding, and appropriate care and treatment afterward. If we're blamed, shamed, or just plain ignored, the effects can be catastrophic.

People often chase these so-called "light bulb moments" where they fully understand some chain of events for the first time. Sometimes I get to see these moments happen right in front of me during a therapy session. A client understands the link between something in their present and something from their past for the first time. They cry, they smile, and they walk out of my office feeling great. Then they walk back in the next week the same person with the same problems. Knowing what made you the way you are doesn't magically undo it. Most of the time, it doesn't do anything at all.

You can drive yourself crazy searching for answers to these questions. Your mind asks them so often and with such urgency that resisting the urge to indulge them can feel nearly impossible. But you'll probably never be able to answer them, and even if you can, it probably won't do anything. I've only found one way out of this cycle; start asking different questions.

Look back on the questions that I began this chapter with, or whatever versions of those questions most frequently run through your mind. Is there anything you notice about them? Anything that stands out to you as problematic?

They're leading questions.

They're all inquiries trying to lead you towards discovering the truth of why you're so bad, stupid, unlovable, or worthless. They all contain assumptions that something about your current existence is problematic, flawed, an issue requiring an explanation. By searching for answers to these questions, you validate their assumptions. You give legitimacy and credence to the idea that there's something seriously wrong with you. You operate on the principle that they are fair, reasonable questions that can lead you to valuable truths.

They aren't. They're just cleverly disguised lies about your self-worth. Ninja insults masquerading as philosophy.

Your mind engages in inquiry naturally, loves to dissect things and seek answers. You can't change that fundamental part of your nature, and you don't necessarily need to. What you need to change are the questions. Instead of continually asking yourself unanswerable questions that chip away at your self-worth, you can start asking questions that have actual answers. Answers that have a chance of leading you out of the never-ending circle of trying to untangle the past.

Instead of "Why am I the way I am?" try asking yourself, "What would help me become more likable to myself?" This adjustment shifts your focus from the past to the present and emphasizes your ability to take action and change whatever it is that you're unhappy with. It can pull you out of thought patterns that encourage feelings of hopelessness and powerlessness. It helps you remember that no matter where you come from, you're the author now, and if you don't like the direction your story is heading in, you can write yourself a new course.

Instead of "Why did that have to happen to me?" try asking yourself, "What would help me recover from what happened to me?" Trying to find rational explanations or a sense of justice for the terrible things you've endured tends to leave you feeling even more frustrated, bitter, angry, and hurt. There usually are no answers. Terrible things happen for no reason, and there isn't always some grand meaning to find. Sometimes things are just awful, and this world can be maddeningly unjust. Your time and energy are better spent on understanding yourself and your needs than seeking some overarching explanation for everything you've suffered.

Instead of "Where did this all go so very wrong?" try asking yourself, "What could make this right?" Shifts like this help you move from feeling like you're a passive observer of your life to an active participant in it. They pull you out of unhelpful rumination and help you focus on solutions. It's pretty hard to see the path forward if you're constantly looking at where you came from.

Instead of "Could things have been different for me?" try asking yourself, "How do I wish things were different for me right now?" Wondering about what could have been is a waste of brainpower. What could you possibly do with an answer to this question, even if you were to find one? Build a time machine so you could go back and change things? Be even more frustrated about the inherent unfairness of life? There's no actionable outcome to answering this question. The emphasis here, again, is focusing on the present and focusing on your power. Your past can never be different. The events that led you to this moment are as unchangeable as always. But the present is malleable. You can change it if you ask yourself the right questions.

You can solve a problem without knowing where the problem came from. You can change a pattern or a bad habit without finding its origin story. If you get a flat tire while driving, do you need to walk back on the road to see what caused the puncture? You'll probably never find it, and even if you do, it doesn't change the fact that you aren't getting home without a new tire. What helps you move forward is being honest and straightforward with yourself about where you are today and where you want to go next. Identify that, and plot a reasonable path to start moving you closer to that place.

Remember This:

Work on catching your train of thought when you notice yourself asking big, unanswerable philosophical questions about life or the world in general and try to redirect that mental energy towards actionable ideas to make your life better today. It's more beneficial to identify what keeps a pattern going in the present than to determine what started it in the past. Your only power is in the current moment. No other timeframes are actionable.

WHEN THE PAST BLEEDS THROUGH

It's so easy to allow your past to have a death grip on your present. Every time someone betrays your trust, manipulates you, ignores you, or intentionally hurts you, it goes into your mental file. You count this file as evidence against all humanity and use it to inform how you participate in all of your future relationships. The hurt you've endured in previous stages of life bleeds through into your daily interactions with others like a gaping wound shoddily covered by a band-aid.

We anticipate that our current or future partners will repeat the hurtful and disrespectful behaviors of past partners. We become hypervigilant for warning signs that we're going to be rejected or abandoned again because the thought terrifies us. We act like the way our parents treated us or each other represents some kind of inevitable truth about love. The more relational wounds we've absorbed in the past, the more we sit on pins and needles waiting for them to show up once more in the present.

These past hurts push us towards extreme ways of being in relationships. Some of us wall ourselves off from the world. We try to be as independent as possible, minimize what we want or need from others, and stay safe in our fortress of solitude. We avoid future pain by never letting ourselves be vulnerable. People can't let us down if we don't want anything from them. Nobody can hurt us if we never let them in. To a degree, it works. Even when relationships crash and burn, your emotional distance from the other person serves as a buffer from the pain.

You also never have the opportunity to be wrong. Another person can't meet your needs if you deny having them. Nobody has the chance to accept you if you don't allow them to know you. Approaching relationships with your walls up and keeping them up no matter what other people show you leads to immense feelings of loneliness and isolation. The world can start to feel like a big, empty tundra. Full of cold, icy things that can't warm you. Living this way isn't freedom from the past; it's allowing your past to imprison your present. It's a retreat inside of yourself.

Some of us go in the opposite direction. We become hypersensitive to rejection and we scan for it constantly. We constantly monitor our relationships with others to look for any signs of rifts, unhappiness, or resentment. If we detect even a hint of disharmony, we instantly blame ourselves and try desperately to fix it. We become passive people pleasers who lack boundaries. We hang on to relationships at any cost, even with toxic or abusive partners, to avoid feelings of abandonment or failure.

We search so hard for signs of problems in our relationships that we see what isn't there. We over-interpret normal disagreements, hear feedback as criticism, and think every argument is a death knell for the relationship. We test people constantly, looking for them to fail our unfair trials as proof that they don't love us, want to leave us, or don't understand us. Sometimes, we even manipulate people into staying with us through deceit or threatened self-destruction.

Some of us adopt the most limiting elements of both coping styles, distancing ourselves from others emotionally while feeling an intense, almost unbearable longing for them. Our relationships take on a detached, insulated quality, like we're observing them through a one-way mirror. Nothing else in the world that feels quite like this. It's like being a living ghost.

What all of these extreme coping strategies have in common is that they create self-fulfilling prophecies. It's these strategies themselves that often cause the breakdowns in our relationships. If people spend enough time with you and pay enough attention to you, they'll notice the walls around your heart. They'll feel the lack of engagement and vulnerability. They'll get tired of being over-analyzed and constantly tested. Eventually they'll leave, and you'll conclude that you were right to be guarded or paranoid, not realizing that your behaviors contributed to the downfall of the relationship. The past then becomes the present as you play out these hurts again and again.

People can never meet your needs if you deny having them, can never show an understanding of your complexity and your humanity if you never let them see anything below your surface. You rob them of the opportunity to independently show you reassurance and appreciation if you continuously seek it out or demand it. If you genuinely want freedom from the past, you can't allow the past to continue to dictate the present. You have to break up with the outdated strategies you've been living by and create something new. Something that serves a purpose beyond dodging pain that's no longer as inevitable or as unbearable as it used to be.

If you've walled yourself off from the world, you'll never escape your past without starting to bring those walls down. They don't have to come down all the way, just far enough that you can emotionally participate in your relationships. Dip a toe in the water now and then. Share something you typically wouldn't let out. Pay very close attention to what happens next. Your belief system will tell you that sharing will lead to hurt, rejection, or misunderstanding, and you might not notice the moments that contradict this belief system unless you look for them.

Being loved or accepted will only help you if you notice that you're loved and accepted. You'll have to train yourself to recognize signs of safety in a relationship. You won't see them if you assume that they don't exist. You might not notice the little moments when somebody legitimately understands and relates to something you've said. You might miss the subtle cues in body language, tone of voice, and facial expression that indicate acceptance and compassion.

If you fall into patterns of desperation and neediness in relationships, you can escape the past by not constantly seeking reassurance from other people. You trap yourself when you try to get ahead of every potential relational rift. How can another person ever earn your trust or prove to you that they care if they're never given a chance because you always get there first? If you pounce on every minor issue like kind sort of relationship cheetah you rob them of the opportunity to show you anything different from what you already know. You have to release people from your cycle to heal your wounds.

Adjacent to moving on from past relational wounds is forgiveness. I often hear forgiveness proposed as a starting point in moving on from being hurt, like there's a switch in your brain you're supposed to find and flip to stop feeling furious, traumatized, or resentful about horrible things that have happened to you. Personally, I've never found that switch. I've only discovered one reliable path to forgiveness; repairing the damage.

I've found that once I recover from whatever pain someone else has caused me, it takes quite a bit of effort for me to hold on to whatever feelings I had towards them. After I patch up and repaint the holes they punched in my walls, the people who wronged me mostly become inconsequential to me. Then, and only then, have I been able to forgive and move on. It's usually the very last domino to fall in that particular chain of events. It's never been the first, at least not for me.

Lastly, we need to talk about apologies. Apologies don't fix anything. Apologies are promises to fix something. If an apology isn't followed by what appears to be a legitimate attempt at making things right again, it probably wasn't a sincere apology. When somebody says "I'm sorry" to you, hear that as "I acknowledge that I've wronged you, and I'm going to try and make it right." You don't have to accept insincere apologies, and you don't have to forgive people just because they've apologized. Being asked to accept an apology from someone who never tries to make things right is like being asked to accept a check from someone in bankruptcy.

Remember This:
Identify and challenge the extreme relational patterns and coping styles you've developed from past interpersonal wounding. Understand how these patterns don't keep you safe from hurt and can become self-fulfilling prophecies that create additional wounding. Be willing to step into discomfort and try relating to others differently than how you've interacted in the past. Don't try to force yourself to forgive the hurts of your past. Instead, try to trust that forgiveness will occur naturally as an outcome of healing and moving forward, rather than being a prerequisite.

TWO PEOPLE PART 2

You'll never feel the way you did when you were a child again.
Not exactly.
Those moments are gone.
Dead, in a sense.
Don't try to go back.
I understand why you want to.
But you can't.
And you can lose your mind trying to.
The person you are today will also die one day.
And the memories of this pain, this isolation, this sense of being completely lost.
One day they'll feel as far away as your childhood does now.
You will become a new creation.
Something with elements of both people.
But someone who is so much more than the sum of their parts.
I know you can't see it now.
And it hurts me that I can't show you.
So much would make sense if I could.
But it doesn't work that way.
Don't try to go back.
There's another escape from where you are.
Go forward.
Don't look for what was lost.
Make something new.
Something you've never seen before.
Something only you can create.
Something with the passion, the love, and the trust that were there early.

But more discerning.
Someone with the fury, the energy, and the discontentment that came later.
But more effective.
Something incomprehensible to the person you are today.

NOBODY KNOWS YOU

You don't really know anyone.

Nobody really knows you.

You think between 60,000 and 80,000 thoughts a day. So does everybody else. You speak around 12,000 words a day. So does everybody else.

Which ideas and experiences are you most likely to verbalize or share on social media? The ones that are most likely to be accepted, praised, and celebrated. Which thoughts and experiences do you think other people are most likely to verbalize or share on social media? The ones that are most likely to be accepted, praised, and celebrated.

What do you think hides amongst the 60,000 or so thoughts that we each choose not to share each day?

Shame.

Failure.

Insecurity.

Regret.

Sorrow.

Embarrassment.

You have access to a tiny fraction of the internal experiences of the people closest to you. That's it. Conversely, you know virtually everything about yourself. Every misstep. Every struggle. Everything you're not proud of.

You cannot compare one person's entire life story, every pitfall, every struggle, every challenge, to another person's highlight reel. And that's all you'll ever have of anyone else's story. The tiny, insignificant pieces that they put out front. The misleading preview they have pre-selected for your viewing.

Don't let yourself take what they show you seriously. It's a masquerade, a costume party. That's all society is. Show this. Hide that. Share this. Keep that to yourself. You do it. I do it. We all do it, and it's essential to know how to do it. But you can't take it to heart. You can't use it as a significant data point for anything. It doesn't mean anything.

The richness of your internal experience is as incomprehensible to other people as theirs is to you. We're all ultimately ignorant about one another. You can never truly know another, and you can never truly be known by another. How could you possibly hope to make a meaningful comparison when the data you need isn't available to you?

You mostly compare yourself as you are today to someone else as they are today. That's a random, arbitrary data point. It doesn't tell you anything useful about the story of each person's life. It's just a single moment in time. Even if this were some kind of race (which it isn't), you can't tell where anyone will finish by taking a snapshot at the halfway mark. Some people sprint right out of the gate and take an early lead, but they can't finish strong. You have a lot of running left to do.

Picture two parallel lines stretching for miles in each direction. One of these lines represents your life, while the other represents the life of whoever you're comparing yourself to at any given moment. When you make that comparison between yourself and someone else, you're looking at a one-inch section of these lines that stretch for hundreds of miles beyond the horizon. What does that single inch tell you about where these lines are heading? Next to nothing. It isn't a useful metric.

There's only one social comparison worth making. Compare the person you are today to the person you were two, three, or four years ago. You know both of those people, and you also know they've had many of the same experiences. This is the closest you can ever have to an accurate comparison between two people.

Even with this, you have to be careful. There may be some elements of your life that look worse today than they did before. Maybe you make less money than you used to. Perhaps you were married and now you're single. These might appear to be steps backward, signs of a downward trend. Your mind will want to focus exclusively on these, point them out to you. Make it look elsewhere as well. Find the progress. Build upon it. Keep taking your next step. It doesn't matter how it compares to someone else's. It's yours, and yours alone.

Remember This:

Try your hardest to stop making inaccurate, arbitrary social comparisons. Instead, try to assess whether you're on track with your personal goals and don't worry about how they "stack up" to whatever anyone else may be doing.

SPECIAL MOMENTS

It's normal to wish that you could go back to a simpler time from your past. It's a lament I frequently hear in therapy sessions. People long for their early, carefree days when they were unburdened by the daily stressors that bury them now. They wish they could just enjoy the present moment and feel as light as they once did.

You can have those feelings again. But you have to understand that the way you're looking at it isn't quite right.

That time from your past that you're thinking of, whatever and whenever it was for you, wasn't any simpler. You were simpler.

My simplest time is a single moment. Sitting on the steps of a laundromat in northern Minnesota on a hot summer day, hearing the sound of the rusty screen door opening and closing as my mother washed load after load of laundry for the three of us while I looked for intriguing rocks in the gravel parking lot. A totally normal moment, unremarkable in every way.

The only explanation I have for why this moment was so special to me is that I was fully present for it. I was dialed in, unburdened by anything other than the weather, the sound of the door, the warmth of the evening summer sun, and the feeling of the rocks in my hands. For that little pocket of time, nothing else mattered. That small laundromat and the gravel parking lot were the entire world as far as I was concerned. Anything beyond my field of vision was outer space. You have your versions of moments like this in your memories. I want to help you make more of them.

Your attention creates your reality. It writes the narrative of your life. You only think about, react to, and remember the parts of your experiences that you pay attention to. Constantly attend to perceptions of threat, and your life feels like endless peril. Constantly attend to feelings of failure, and your life feels like infinite despair. You can have everything in the world, and it will feel like nothing if you don't mentally engage with it.

That's why people can have what seems to be a great life on the outside and still be deeply unhappy. Having anything in life, whether it's a fantastic spouse, beautiful kids, a great career, a spiritual calling, or the house of your dreams, won't make any difference in your overall life satisfaction if you don't force your mind to take notice of it from time to time.

You're constantly surrounded by more stimuli than you can attend to, even during the calm, quiet, under-stimulating moments of your life. Your brain automatically selects a small cross-section of what's happening around you and presents it for conscious interpretation. As an organ that prioritizes safety and threat identification, your brain tends to select the most damaging, threatening, or unsatisfying elements of your present experience. It's sort of an anti-highlight reel. It wants you to see all of the worst parts of your life and keep your focus on them. It's scared that an unseen danger might blindside you, that there's some hidden threat out there waiting to take you down.

Think of your attention as being represented by a pie chart. Very rarely is 100% of your attention focused entirely on one thing; you're almost always divided to some extent. The biggest pieces of the pie will represent your memories and your narrative of a specific time or experience. It doesn't matter what's happening around you. All that matters is what makes up your pie.

That's how special moments pass you by every day. They don't announce themselves as special, and you can so easily miss them when you're distracted. When you reflect upon your special memories, you'll notice they're a blend of the obvious highlights of your life and many seemingly mundane or routine experiences. What made the mundane into the memorable wasn't the experience; it was your attention. You were there. Not just physically, but mentally. You weren't wondering about tomorrow. You weren't ruminating about yourself. You were all in, locked into that moment, living it with your entire being. And you can do it again.

Here's an example of how your special moments disappear. It's early spring, and you've just received a subpar performance review at work. After you get home, you go for a walk to clear your head. It's a beautiful day, high 60s and sunny. There's a light, pleasant breeze. The birds are singing enthusiastically, and the flowers are just beginning to bloom. The world smells fresh and alive as it emerges from the silence of the winter months. As you're walking, an eagle flies over your head. Thirty feet to your right, a deer watches you from the brush. You spend the walk ruminating on your performance at work over the past year. "What should I have done differently?" "Am I going to get fired if I can't turn this around?" "Why am I so lazy?" Your attention is turned inward to a potential thread.

You won't remember the weather, or the birds, or the deer. You'll barely remember this day at all, and the memory that stands out the most will be the performance review. You can only recall what you attend to. Your attention wasn't directed towards the beauty around you, so the beauty that was all around you didn't become part of your story. This day becomes just another chapter of anxiety, failure, and sadness.

When you try to force your mind to spend more time on pleasant elements of your experiences, it may rebel against you. "But what about all of the DOOM?" it will ask you. "What about the DEATH and the DESTRUCTION and the DISASTER? What will happen if we stop worrying about these things if we don't constantly prepare for them?"

It's a fair question. It deserves an answer.

First, roughly what percentage of the doom scenarios come to fruition? Maybe a few occasionally, but most never happen, at least not in the way you fear that they will. Second, how much does your pre-stressing about them help you? Maybe you're a little less surprised when they happen, but they're still incredibly painful, and you still have to handle the fallout.

Spending too much time in the past or the future steals the present away from you. You miss most of your special moments. The life you've worked so hard to build flies right past you under your radar. Logically, you know your quality of life is at least decent, but you just don't feel it. All you notice is the negative.

One of the most effective ways to spend more time in the present moment is to intentionally tune in to your five senses; sight, smell, taste, touch, and sound. Reflect on any strong memory, and you'll notice a wealth of sensory data around that memory. The smell of the ocean. The cold breeze of a winter morning with a warm cup of coffee in your hand. The taste of your favorite meal at your favorite restaurant. The posters you had on your wall as a teenager. Even reading these simple depictions probably evokes rich, plentiful memories for you. Memories created in large part by sensory information.

Your senses are always 100% present. They are interpreted by your hindbrain, a part of the brain that doesn't hold conscious thoughts or episodic memories. They're untainted by your insecurities, your emotional baggage, your pain. They're pure information about this exact moment, and that's all they're ever capable of being. They're your secret to staying present, making new memories, and appreciating the beautiful things you already have. They are your anchors in the turbulent sea of your mind. Use them often.

If your mind is fighting you particularly hard on staying present, consider incorporating an anchoring phrase. An anchoring phrase is an internal self-statement, almost like a mantra, that you can use to train yourself to return to the present moment. Pairing this statement repeatedly with other present-focused psychological practices like tuning in to your senses establishes a neurological pathway that strengthens your ability to tune out the past and the future. I use "special moment alert" for my anchoring statement.

Remember This:

Practice consciously directing your attention to the stimuli, experiences, and memories you want to be the defining moments of your life. Use your awareness to write your narrative. Practice tuning into your five senses and using an anchoring statement to keep your mind from wandering too far into the past or the future.

PEOPLE LIKE ME

Why can't I find people like me?
Why make only one of something?
I feel like the last of my species.
Why create me just to torment me?
Why must you show me, every day, the things I don't have?
You place it all around me.
But you give none of it to me.
Where are you?
Are you out there somewhere?
Why can't I see you?
I'm looking.
Searching.
Shining my dim spotlight into every dark corner.
Looking in places I have no business traveling to.
Crawling through sewers and basements.
Doing things I should never do.
My soul has no home anymore.

GRATITUDE TAKES PRACTICE

"Just be thankful for everything you have."

"Try to appreciate the little things."

"Practicing gratitude is crucial for mental health."

Great. How?

Gratitude really is tremendously important, but telling someone to be grateful doesn't make them grateful. Using ineffective gratitude practices to try and force yourself to feel something that isn't there can make you feel worse. I've never seen anyone acknowledge this, but I've felt it.

The first potential problem is self-invalidation. Sometimes we identify a source of gratitude and then instantly turn it around on ourselves and use it as a source of shame for whatever painful emotions we might be experiencing. In other words, this:

"I am grateful that my heart is healthy."

Turns into this:

"I am grateful that my heart is healthy; therefore, I should not be upset about the health problems that I do have because other people have heart problems."

We like to turn life into a sorrow competition, and only the "winner" gets to be upset about anything. The rest of us are just supposed to be happy that we aren't that person. Unless you have literally the worst life in the world, you're just supposed to keep calm and carry on.

This is stupid.

Each person has an inner ten-point emotional pain scale. The worst thing that's ever happened to you is your ten. It doesn't matter how your ten objectively compares to someone else's ten. It doesn't change your scale when you learn about awful things you've never experienced. What you feel is based on your personal emotional pain scale and nothing more.

If you were to witness my 8-year-old-son's reaction to being asked to do his homework without knowing him, you might think that a loved one has just died. It's easily a solid 8 for him. He's had a good life. Someday he'll become aware of the horrors that some children face, like abuse and neglect. Because he won't experience these things firsthand, they won't modify his scale. They may give him some sense of perspective that he can use to calm himself, but they won't change his pain. His pain being about something that looks small to me doesn't make it any less real to him.

I also see people getting stuck in their attempts at gratitude practice by being too vague or general. You'll be more able to access gratitude if you're as specific as possible about what you're grateful for. Broad statements about life don't make us feel much of anything because they don't attach to anything or conjure up specific memories or experiences. For example, try to do this:

"I am grateful for the vacation we took last summer."

And not this:

"I am grateful that I have a good life."

The first statement relates to a specific experience or set

of experiences that you've had recently. When thinking about a vacation you've taken, your mind will recall some of the highlights of that vacation, and you'll have an emotional reaction to those memories. Assuming they're pleasant memories, they should automatically connect to a feeling of gratitude most of the time.

The second statement is just too general. It's more likely to trigger rumination or arguing with yourself than gratitude. What does it mean to have a good life? Do you actually have a good life? What about the bad parts? If you have a good life, but you don't feel constant gratitude about it, are you actually being ungrateful? It's so easy to get stuck in these thoughts.

You also don't have to limit your gratitude practice to elements of your life that are specific to you. We often ask, "what's so special about my life or my experiences?" when attempting to practice gratitude, but it's just as important to be thankful for things most of us or all of us have. There are so many parts of our daily lives that seem ordinary or mundane because we're too used to them. If you try to look at them with alien eyes, eyes that don't understand the miracles surrounding us every day, you may find an unexpected well of gratitude.

Take electricity, for example. Flipping a switch and turning on a light probably doesn't blow your mind on a daily basis, but it absolutely should. If you truly consider the process that has to happen to create that reaction, it's absolutely incredible.

First, electricity is produced by a generating station which a group of people had to build. Generating stations convert natural resources like wind, water, and coal into electrical power that humans can use. Then that electricity is sent to a transformer to increase the voltage, allowing it to travel from the generating station to businesses and neighborhoods without fizzling out. It then travels from the transformer to a substation, a routing point to distribute it to the proper locations. The electricity is sent to another transformer from the substation to reduce the voltage and make it safe for home use. Then it enters your home through a meter, connects to your breaker box to further ensure safety, and finally travels to your switches and outlets. And when you flip that switch and your light bulbs turn on, that's what happened behind the scenes to make it work.

How is that not amazing? And that's one example of thousands. You're surrounded by incredible processes like this every day. Plumbing. Human language. The position of the earth relative to the sun. These miracles aren't unique to you, but that doesn't make them any less special. Your life is full of wonder if you'll allow yourself to see it.

Remember This:
To really feel gratitude as an emotion and not just a thought exercise, be as specific and as detailed as possible with yourself about what you are grateful for. Try to avoid broad, vague expressions of gratitude that don't connect with particular thoughts, feelings, or memories. Don't use your gratitude about your life to invalidate or shame yourself.

DOES IT MAKE ME FASTER?

I was a senior in high school when "The Fast And The Furious" came out. It was a dark era for my friends and me. We already liked driving fast and modifying our cars before Paul Walker and Vin Diesel made it look good. My friends did anyway. I mostly just hung out and pretended to understand what they were talking about. My Pontiac Grand Am wasn't going to be fast no matter what I did to it.

After that movie came out, the car aftermarket became flooded with cosmetic modifications. Giant spoilers. Underbody neon lights. Car culture had become trendy. Knowing what we wanted from our cars was crucial, because performance modifications and cosmetic modifications cancel each other out to a degree. The "upgrades" that made your car look faster tended to make it slower because of the added weight and decreased aerodynamics. I saw a lot of people drop a lot of money on a mix of performance parts and cosmetic parts and end up with a car that functioned about the same as it did before they started putting money into it. Car modifications can quickly become a net-zero equation.

I see this happen to people in all areas of life. They aren't able to be specific enough about what they want most, and they end up trying to have a little bit of everything. Sometimes these desires cancel each other out. Sometimes we feel bored and make changes that we think will bring excitement into our lives, only to find that those "exciting" changes end up being stressors, and what we really wanted was peace.

To stay on track with our cars, we developed what I now understand to have been an anchoring phrase; "Does it make me faster?" We didn't want to get sucked into the trend of making our cars pretty. We just wanted to go fast. This question helped us resist the temptation to buy all of the flashy new products that were suddenly available. Does a new cold air intake make me faster? Yes! Buy one and install it. Does a giant spoiler on the back of my car make me faster? No! Don't buy it. Do my floor mats make me faster? No! Get them out of there. We had a manifesto, and we followed the manifesto.

Having a clear sense of direction is essential if you want to have any chance of getting what you want from this life. I know how overwhelming your choices can be. There's a near-infinite configuration of majors, career paths, cities, partners, and hobbies. The idea that you can be anything you want isn't always freeing; sometimes it's just confusing and stressful, like trying to commit to a new show on Netflix. That's why I encourage people to set goals based more on how they want to feel than on who they want to be. If you know what you want to feel more of, it should narrow down your choices significantly.

Just don't say that you want to be "happy." It's not specific enough. Happy and unhappy aren't emotions; they're categories of emotions. We use the word "happy" to describe a diverse range of pleasant feelings like joy, peace, excitement, love, and accomplishment. We use "unhappy" to express unpleasant emotions like fear, loneliness, sadness, irritability, frustration, and betrayal, and the general absence of positive emotions. These terms are too broad to provide a sense of direction. Saying you want to be "happy" is like saying you want someone to paint your house "blue." It gives general guidance, but if you're picturing a navy blue house and I paint it neon blue, you probably won't be very "happy."

That's why you need to be as specific as possible. For most of us, some pleasant feelings feel more enjoyable than others. Personally, I'm an achievement guy. Nothing feels quite as good to me as setting a goal and checking it off my list. That's why I wrote a book. If I were an excitement guy I wouldn't have written a book because, let me tell you, it's not a very exciting process save for a few highlights. But it makes me "happy" because that's the type of person I am.

Try to figure out which feelings feel best to you. Do you generally prefer excitement or peace? Do you generally prefer freedom or achievement? They aren't necessarily oppositional to one another, but knowing which you prefer can provide tremendous guidance on some of the tough choices we're faced with, like who to partner with and what to do for a living. You can turn your favorite feeling into an anchoring question too, like we did with our cars. If you're a peace person, asking yourself, "will this make me feel more at peace?" when you're faced with a tough choice can help guide you in the right direction.

If identifying your feelings is hard for you, please use this chart to help you be as specific as possible:

Joy

Feels Like: An emotional version of warm sunshine. Lightness, smiling, and laughter. Easygoing, exciting engagement.

Created By: Fun, low stress, energetic activities.

Examples: Going out with friends. Watching a funny movie. Sharing a memorable childhood experience with your children. Spending a few hours at the beach.

Pride/Accomplishment/Competency/Fulfillment

Feels Like: Being bigger, stronger, and better than you were before. "Leveling up" in life.

Created By: Creating things. Finishing things. Learning new

skills. Overcoming challenges and insecurities.

Examples: Finishing a home improvement project. Reading an educational book or article. Cleaning or organizing part of your house. Working out. Finishing a project for work.

Excitement/Optimism/Hope

Feels Like: Positive energy propelling you forward. A desire to see what happens next and a belief that it could be great.

Created By: Having or planning things to look forward to.

Examples: Planning a vacation. Scheduling a date night or an outing with friends. Signing up to take a class for fun.

Love/Connection/Belonging/Intimacy

Feels Like: A warm and fuzzy feeling in your heart. Being "at home" around other people.

Created By: Opening up to safe people. Being vulnerable and feeling validated. Spending quality time on a shared interest with others.

Examples: Going on a date. Telling someone a secret. Talking about your day.

Peace/Contentment

Feels Like: Your stress is taking some time off. Your brain is moving a little more slowly.

Created By: Distracting from stress. Engaging your parasympathetic nervous system.

Examples: Meditation. Spiritual resources. Spending time in nature. Deep breathing. Progressive muscle relaxation. Yoga. Aromatherapy. Massage.

Remember This:

Most people have one or two feelings that generally feel better to them than other enjoyable feelings. Try

to figure out what your preferred feelings are and use that knowledge to guide your choices in life.

PEOPLE LIKE ME PART 2

There are no people like you.
There aren't supposed to be.
You are a collision of matter and soul.
This version of a person has never existed before.
It will never exist again after you're gone.
It won't even exist tomorrow.
You are a new being each morning, shaped by the events of the previous day.
Every interaction you have with someone tomorrow will be a novel, irreplaceable experience to them.
Every action you will take tomorrow has never happened before and will never happen again. Not in the exact way it will happen tomorrow.
Stop searching the darkest recesses of life.
Looking for something that's been by your side.
Shine that light inside.
Get to know what resides within.
Don't look for yourself in broken places.
Don't just wake up tomorrow morning.
Don't crawl out of bed, already defeated.
Rise up tomorrow morning.
Show the world something it's never seen before.
The way only you can.

IT'S ALL ABOUT LOVE

"You just need to learn to love yourself!"

Another theoretical cure-all. An obnoxiously frequent response to any self-disclosure around insecurity, low self-esteem, poor body image, and other adjacent topics. An empty idea rarely followed by actionable strategies.

Genuine self-love is invaluable, but people who haven't struggled with self-loathing don't understand how wide the gap is between having it and lacking it. They speak of self-love like it's an exit you missed on the highway, like all you need to do is turn back and remember to take it this time. There's no switch to flip in your brain to activate all of your missing feelings towards yourself. As with so many things involving the mind, it's less of a simple adjustment and more of a complete reprogramming.

I once knew someone who was exceptionally wealthy. Think "garage full of various Ferraris" wealthy. I was absolutely awestruck by his collection. I'll never forget his response when I asked which of his eight cars was his favorite.

It was his 1994 Mazda RX-7 parked on the street.

I was baffled. A mid 90's RX-7 is a great car, but it was the worst car he owned by every possible metric. It was the slowest, the oldest, the least valuable, the least luxurious, and the most common. I couldn't wrap my head around what he was telling me, so I asked some follow-up questions. I needed to understand this.

What I eventually came to understand was that he felt

more connected with his RX-7 than with any of his other cars. Because it was a relatively simple and inexpensive car, he worked on it himself. He changed his own oil, rotated his own tires, and generally served as the car's mechanic. He had made some simple cosmetic and performance upgrades to it, nothing that dramatically altered the car, just simple and fun projects. He genuinely felt like the RX-7 was "his" and something he enjoyed taking care of. He described it as feeling almost like an extension of himself.

The Ferraris, meanwhile, were too complicated and too expensive for him to feel comfortable working on them. He loved driving them, but that's where his relationship with them ended. He didn't feel connected to them in the same way because he wasn't the one who cared for them or improved them. His financial investment in the Ferraris was exponentially greater, but his investment of time, energy, and emotion into his RX-7 was what mattered most to him. He liked his Ferrari collection, but the only car he truly loved was the RX-7.

I ruminated on that conversation for weeks before I finally felt like I understood it. I used my understanding of this experience to create a theory, an idea which I've tested time and time again with my therapy clients and in my personal life. So far, it's never been contradicted, and it was an absolutely life-changing revelation.

My theory is that the extent to which we care about something, love something, and appreciate something is based primarily on our investment of time, energy, and emotion into that thing. I think that our love for things has nothing to do with the "objective" quality of that thing. I believe that we can only love things if we treat them with love, no matter how wonderful they may be. And that includes our feelings towards ourselves.

We like to set standards for self-love.

"I'll love myself if I get down to a certain weight or a specific size."

"I'll love myself if I get that promotion or make a certain amount of money."

"I'll love myself if somebody else loves me."

I'm completely convinced that accomplishments like these are worthless and arbitrary as far as self-love goes. They don't do anything. Check all the boxes you want, but none of these will magically make you love yourself, even if you do manage to achieve them. You can turn yourself into a Ferrari, but it won't matter if you don't treat yourself with love.

It's hard to love something if you don't invest in it. Our time, our energy, and our emotions are our most precious resources. When we consistently devote them to something or someone, it sends a clear signal to our brain; "This is important to me." The more you invest, the more important the object of your investment becomes to you. You can't force yourself to love yourself through sheer mental willpower, but you can train yourself to love yourself by investing in yourself. Regular, simple investments seem to be the most effective for most people. Human versions of oil changes and tire rotations. Here are some examples:

- Spending extra time on grooming, hair, makeup, and wardrobe to show yourself that you value your appearance.
- Journaling about your feelings, then reading your journal to show yourself that you care about your feelings.
- Checking in with yourself physically and mentally throughout your day to show yourself that you're emotionally invested in your own well-being.
- Devoting time to self-care each day through exercise, yoga, meditation, or spiritual practices to show yourself that you care about your health.

- Doing one thing to improve your self-confidence each day, such as practicing a new skill to show yourself that you're worth your own time.
- Purchasing clothes and self-care products for yourself that are a little more expensive and luxurious than what you typically allow to show yourself that you matter.

I like to stick with little daily investments like these. You might think that big, grandiose gestures towards yourself would be even more effective. Taking a week off from work to treat yourself to a dream vacation, for example. But I think our relationships with ourselves generally follow the same guidelines as our interactions with other people. Most of us would prefer to be with someone who consistently treats us with love, respect, and dignity than to be with someone who occasionally rides in on a white stallion to love bomb us with some over-the-top gesture then disappears for weeks. Don't love bomb yourself.

Make investments in yourself that will lift you up every day, and enjoy the compound interest your investments bring. Like growing a retirement fund, the progress may be slow and somewhat erratic from one day to the next, but it will be steady over time.

Remember This:

Work on facilitating feelings of love and appreciation for yourself by investing more of your time, energy, and emotions into yourself. Focus on small, habitual details of your day rather than big, one-off experiences. Train your mind to regard you as important, valuable, and worth investing resources into through your daily actions.

PAIN AND PURPOSE

You have at least one special gift. I can't claim to know what it is, but I do know that you have one. We all do. Our gifts are fond of hiding, and they're particularly attracted to hiding underneath pain. These gifts are skills or traits that not just everybody has, and so they make us stand out or feel different in some way. Sometimes they draw unwanted attention to ourselves, so we try to hide or mask them in various ways. Being different isn't always celebrated. It can be painful. Other people might not like how we're different and might not be shy about letting us know that.

My special gift is empathy. Almost everyone has empathy, but I was born with too much of it. In childhood and adolescence, it made my life horrible at times. I was utterly unable to handle the idea of anyone or anything suffering. My parents had to be extra careful that I didn't catch so much as a glimpse of the news, or I'd have an emotional crisis that might last all night long. Most children's movies had way too much adversity for me to be able to tolerate. I used to harass my dad to release the fish he planned to keep and cook until he inevitably let them go. I was emotionally unable to handle seeing them confined in the fish basket, bound for death via filet knife.

If anything I do seems extraordinary to you, it's only because I've embraced my gift while you may still be hiding yours. You don't have to do it anymore. You can create safety for yourself, can build distance from those who judge, hate, or harm you for what makes you special. If you're having trouble finding it, look for where your pain is. It's probably hiding under that.

Finding and using your special gift is so important if you want to win this war with yourself. No matter how objectively good your life may be, how well you take care of yourself, or how many beautiful things you may have, nihilism can always sabotage you. You can be in the midst of your gratitude practice, genuinely thankful for all that you have, when your brain shows its trump card; "but what if none of that matters?" Without a sense of meaning, everything you've been working for can still leave you feeling hollow and empty inside.

That hollow feeling is incredibly dangerous. When we do things that generally make us feel excited, joyful, or peaceful, and instead, we feel nothing, our brains become confused. They anticipate a feeling that never comes. This often gets us into feedback loops or leads to destructive behaviors as we chase a feeling we aren't physically capable of experiencing at the moment. You might end up binge-watching a show for hours because you aren't experiencing the humor or excitement you expect. You might end up getting drunk because even 10 hours of watching the funniest show you know of didn't make you laugh once, and you're desperate just to feel something, anything.

Meaning is the counter to nihilism, a vaccination against the hollowness. It fills a part of you that nothing else can fill. It gives you an unshakeable, rock-solid foundation of purpose. It refreshes you. It gives you energy, drive, and focus on the days when such things would otherwise be absent.

Your purpose doesn't have to be a religious practice. It certainly can be, but that's not a requirement. Some find it more accessible, more sustainable, more believable to follow a system that's already in place, something that's been a part of humanity for thousands of years. Others find that none of these systems fit them quite right, and they need something more tailored to them specifically. Neither of these is right or wrong, good or bad. The only spiritually "bad" position to be in is to lack meaning and purpose.

Anything you do can be spiritual if it connects to some kind of calling or meaning for you. If you're a parent who had a difficult childhood, raising your children can be a spiritual practice. What could be more meaningful than creating safety and joy for people who can't make their own?

Your career can be spiritual. Every occupation plays a vital role in the functioning of our social system. Some of these roles are more celebrated than others, more fairly compensated than others, but you don't have to align with the general social perspective of your career. I know someone whose sense of purpose comes from creating habitats for ducks. It can be literally anything.

Art can be spiritual. Painting. Writing. Music. Dancing. Ways of expressing your unique patterns of thought, the special ways that you see the world. Anything that connects you with others or allows you to help others.

Look back. Find it. Reclaim it. Use it.

Remember This:
Reclaim what's different or special about you and find ways to incorporate it into your day, whether in your profession or your personal life. Remember that anything that connects to a sense of purpose or spirituality fills the hollow, and almost anything you do can be spiritual. Don't let anyone but you define your purpose.

THE BAT CAVE

We went to the bat cave again today.
That old storm sewer that you can walk through.
An extension of the creek running through a hill.
Miles of winding, twisting concrete caverns.
Running below streets, parking lots, and a graveyard.
Gradually becoming narrower.
Water constantly deepening. Starting at the ankles. Working its way to the waist.
Pitch black even during the day.
Every quarter mile or so, there was a large concrete pipe.
We tried to move one once, just for fun. Four healthy teenage boys. We couldn't manage it.
We concluded that the pipes were immobile.
About a half-mile in, our only flashlight died.
We turned around to head back, no choice but to hold hands or risk getting lost.
Then we heard it.
The unmistakable sound of concrete scraping concrete.
Chills.
Silence.
A second scrape.
A pipe was moving.
Panic.
Terror.
Running.
Falling.
Bruises.
Cuts.

Screaming.
Cursing.
And then…daylight.
All four of us had made it out.
Each a bloody mess.
We never spoke of it again.
I'm sure, somehow, it had a logical explanation.
But I still don't know what that would be.
Something just as strange happened to me the following day.
I felt decent.
Not great, but decent.
I hadn't felt decent in a long time.
Maybe I'm a little more attached to being alive than I thought.

I LOVE DISCOMFORT

Your nervous, conservative, and survivalist mind encourages you to avoid discomfort. "What if it hurts?" says the mind. "What if it's embarrassing?" "What if you aren't good at it?" "What if it doesn't work?" I want you to know that discomfort is not your enemy. Not even close. Discomfort is a map to buried treasure. It is the most straightforward set of directions you will ever receive on what you need to do to feel stronger, more intelligent, more capable, more confident, and less afraid. All you have to do is embrace it.

Right now, you have a comfort zone. You have a particular set of tasks, people, places, and activities that almost always feel safe to you. You can do these things, visit these places, or see these people with minimal anxiety and preparation.

There are also tasks, people, places, and activities that feel completely overwhelming to you. Things that are just too much for the current version of you to handle. There will always be parts of your life that fall into this category, and that's fine. Nobody is a master of everything. These are things you currently prefer to avoid at all costs.

I want you to be on the lookout for things that fall into the narrow sliver of space between your comfort zone and the overwhelming space. You'll know you've found something in this space when you feel uneasy, uncertain, ambivalent, and nervous, but NOT like you're on the verge of a panic attack. I call this area your discomfort zone.

Accessing your discomfort zone is like stretching the

muscles of your mind. If you wanted to be more physically flexible, you'd have to regularly stretch your muscles to the point of physical discomfort. That discomfort, that stretch just beyond your normal range of motion, is where the growth and flexibility are created. If you halt the stretch before you feel uncomfortable, you don't challenge your body enough for it to improve. If you barrel right past your feelings of discomfort and try to do the splits, you'll pull your groin and you won't stretch again for six months because of the painful memory of your pulled groin. Don't pull your groin.

Discomfort cannot last forever in the absence of some actual threat or problem. An anxiety response is a very taxing state for your mind and body to be in, and they can't sustain it indefinitely without some type of external reinforcer. In other words, as long as nothing truly terrible happens to you, your discomfort will begin to fade. You just have to hang in there long enough to get over that first hill of anxiety. Most discomfort is not a sign that something is dangerous, harmful, or problematic. It's usually just an indicator that what you're doing is unfamiliar. When the unfamiliar becomes familiar, the discomfort begins to fade.

After you spend enough time in your discomfort zone, it becomes a part of your comfort zone. When this happens, your comfort zone becomes larger, the amount of things in this world that overwhelm you shrinks, and your discomfort zone levels up. What previously felt uncomfortable now feels comfortable, and what once felt overwhelming now feels merely uncomfortable. When this happens, recalibrate to find your new discomfort zone and keep going.

Don't miss the enormity of what you can do using this. It's a simple strategy, but it's unbelievably powerful. Can you imagine what it would feel like if most things in life were in your comfort zone? If it was very, very difficult for the world to throw something at you that would even stand a chance of disrupting you? You can have this. You can BE this. There isn't much of a limit to how far you can take this as long as you're willing to be patient with yourself.

I'll show you a specific example of how this can play out. Let's say you have a fear of driving. Here's where we would start:

Comfort zone: Being in a car when someone else is driving.

Discomfort zone: Sitting in the driver's seat of a car that isn't running.

We want you to spend some time in your discomfort zone every day. For maybe 15 or 20 minutes, you'd sit in the driver's seat of a car that isn't running. Initially, this will be tough for you. Eventually, maybe after a week or two, your anxiety reaction will start to decrease as your mind becomes more comfortable with, and accepting of, this situation. When this no longer feels challenging, sitting in the driver's seat is now a part of your comfort zone. This means your discomfort zone has moved again, and we have to recalibrate. Perhaps the next step looks something like this:

Comfort Zone: Sitting in the driver's seat of a car that isn't running.

Discomfort Zone: Sitting in the driver's seat of a running, parked car.

The car is running now, which adds a lot of new stimuli to the situation. Your brain now has to take in the sound of the engine, the vibration in your chair, and the lights on the dashboard being illuminated. It will need some time to acclimate to this, and we will give it time. When this becomes comfortable, we recalibrate again.

Comfort Zone: Sitting in the driver's seat of a running, parked car.

Discomfort Zone: Backing down the driveway, then back

into the driveway.

You continue this process until, eventually, you're driving on the highway. It might take a year, and that's fine. If you get impatient with yourself and try to push past your discomfort zone too quickly, you might overwhelm yourself and avoid everything driving-related for months. Patience is the key. As long as you're on a trajectory of growth, you'll eventually reach your goal. Don't push yourself too hard. It's completely counterproductive.

It's so easy to look at how far away you are from your goals and want to give up. I know the feeling of looking up towards the life you want to live and seeing what looks like miles and miles of unscalable cliffs, an absolute mountain between you and your dreams. It's just that, most of the time, the individual steps to get from here to there aren't that difficult. It's looking at them all at once that feels overwhelming, but you won't be doing it all at once. You have your entire life to climb that mountain, and if you don't get all the way to the top, so what? Every step is something to be proud of.

Remember This:

Seek out experiences that push you slightly past your current comfort zone to expand it. This helps you feel safer and more confident. Make sure to move forward at a measured pace. If you never push yourself, you can't grow stronger and more comfortable. If you push yourself too hard, you'll decompensate and fall backward. Work on discerning between the moments when you need a little nudge forward and the moments when you need everyone, including yourself, to back off and dial down the pressure.

RELEASE IT

You have a built-in security system. A series of alarms and monitors that activate when something seems amiss. When your security system goes off, you get that racing-heart, hard-to-breathe, sweaty, shaky, nauseous, dizzy, senses-heightened, tight muscles feeling. We all have those reactions from to time. Some of us have them much more often than others.

The more frightening and disturbing experiences you've had in your life, the more heightened your security system becomes. It adds neurological cameras, motion sensors, tripwires, and glass break alarms. It can become so sensitive that it frequently triggers in response to everyday life events. Living with near-constant alarm bells going off inside of you is nerve-wracking.

I had a friend growing up whose family had an extremely high-end home security system. It was a problem. Drop your fork on your plate, and you'd trigger the kitchen glass break alarm. Vibrations from the wind on blustery days would trigger the break-in sensors. There were typically 2 or 3 false alarms a day. I always felt on edge at his place, wondering when the next alert was coming.

Being a person with an upgraded mental security system feels a lot like this. Even when you're safe, you don't feel safe. It's always just a matter of time before the alarm goes off, and it's so hard to fully relax into a moment when you know you could be jolted out of it at any time.

There's a common saying that people only use 10% of

their brains. It's a half-truth. We use about 10% of our brains at any given time. We use our entire brain throughout the day, but it has a power grid-like ability to reallocate resources depending on what we're doing. Work on a complex math problem, and your logical, rational functions activate. Work on an art project, and your creative, emotional side comes to the forefront.

When your internal alarm system is triggered, the 10% of your brain that activates are the parts that are ready for war. Adrenaline spikes. Senses heighten. Conscious, rational thought fades to the back of your mind. Sometimes you get loud, angry, tearful, and shaky. Other times you're rigid, quiet, tense, and withdrawn. Sometimes you might be a mix of both. This is you in war mode.

When the war doesn't come, the tension and energy remain unused. They stay stuck in your body, cycling over and over again, waiting for the mortal threat that rarely manifests. Most of the daily terrors we face pose no physical threat. You have to speak publicly. Someone you love may be mad at you. That bill was higher than usual, and you aren't sure how you'll pay it this month.

You never get to run from these stressors. You can't fight them with your body. These battles play out in your mind and only in your mind. Your body sits on the sidelines, ready for action, primed with adrenaline in anticipation of doing whatever it needs to do to keep you safe.

Your nervous system needs to release this built-up energy to feel safe again. That's the signal that all is well. When you've put the pent-up energy to good use, your nervous system assumes that you either fought off the threat or fled to safety. If you haven't used the energy, it assumes you must still be in danger.

Therein lies the trick. You have to find a way to use that

energy. You have to convince your nervous system and your limbic system that the stressors have passed so that you can move on with your day.

The next time you experience a false alarm, find an outlet for the energy it creates. My favorite is pushing. Choose an object that's either extremely heavy or entirely immobile. Walls are great for this. Large pieces of furniture work. People can work, as long as you remember to acquire their consent before pushing them. Push slowly, intentionally, mindfully, and firmly against the object, as if you're rolling a boulder up a hill. Don't use fast, forceful, or jerky movements. You don't want to break anything, particularly yourself.

If you're in a situation where pushing furniture around the room would draw unwanted attention, progressive muscle relaxation is a great substitution. In most cases, people won't even notice that you're doing it. Intentionally tighten your most activated muscle groups, one by one, beyond their already wound-up point. Hold that increased tension for a few seconds, then release it. Repeat this a few times for each muscle group, then move on to the next area where you feel tight. The additional tension you create simulates an actual use of physical energy in a way that often tricks your body into thinking you've either fought off the threat or escaped from it.

Deep breathing is the other practice you'll want to familiarize yourself with if false alarms are a frequent occurrence for you. Slowing and deepening our breath allows us to speak with a part of our bodies that we don't typically have the chance to communicate with; the nervous system. Your nervous system regulates many of your autonomous physiological processes like breathing, heart rate, blood pressure, digestion, and collecting and processing sensory inputs. All of these processes run automatically, but breath has the unique distinction of being the only autonomous nervous system function that you can consciously take control of.

Your nervous system lacks language receptors; it doesn't understand positive self-talk, mantras, or cognitive-behavioral therapy. That's why using these strategies often calms your mind but not your body, and you logically know you're going to be fine but your body continues to panic. Your only way to get your body to calm down is to speak its language; the language of controlled breathing.

You might hear a lot of advice on how, exactly, you should practice deep breathing. Some people say to hold your breath, some say not to. Some say a breath should be 4 seconds, some say it should be 8. Some say the exhale should be longer than the inhale, others say they should be the same. Don't worry about it. Your nervous system doesn't care which technique you use. Slower, deeper breathing sends a signal from your conscious mind to your autonomic physiological processes that all is well. That's the only part you need to know and remember. I've always found it incredibly counter-productive to complicate interventions that are meant to reduce stress. Keep it simple, and use whatever technique or style feels right for you.

Remember This:
We experience a lot of "false alarms" in life, especially those of us who have had a lot of true alarms. Your body needs to be allowed to release the energy it stores during these false alarms and return to a calm, restful state. You can accomplish this by pushing, using progressive muscle relaxation, and practicing deep breathing techniques.

THE BAT CAVE PART 2

You're going to experience a lot of things that defy explanation in your life.
Confusing, bizarre, nonsensical, terrifying things.
Sometimes it will appear that nobody else notices them.
Which will scare you even more.
It's a lonely way to live.
Being the only one to feel certain things.
Feeling like you have two sets of emotions.
The normal human responses.
And the feelings with no names.
The feelings that are more like pictures.
The ones you can't communicate to others.
Without learning an alien language.
Some day you'll use all of it.
Like the native Americans used every part of the buffalo.
Even the disgusting, unappetizing, seemingly useless parts.
It all has a purpose.
You can't even begin to imagine the intricacy of the story you're writing.

NEUROLOGICAL SUPERBEING

If you want to take good care of your brain, you can't neglect your body. Your body regulates your brain's ability to access the resources it needs to do its best work. It's the provider of the oxygen, energy, blood, and rest that keep your mind sharp. If your brain is even mildly deprived of just one of these crucial resources, you will feel it. You won't be able to think as clearly or make choices as effectively. You will feel slower, foggier, and heavier. Everything you do will require more effort. Your emotions will be less regulated, more erratic.

I know that caring for your physical body is a lot to ask when you're feeling down, hopeless, lethargic, or just plain stressed. I get that being physically active when you feel like absolute crap is tremendously unappealing. Just know that it's one of the fastest and most foolproof ways to help you feel better. The neurological changes that occur after physical activity are somewhat akin to a cocktail of the most effective psychiatric medications on the market with faster symptom reduction and zero side effects. The psychological benefits of exercise are so incredible they aren't appropriate for paragraph form and require bullet points:

- Stressors feel less stressful. People rate the same situations lower on a subjective stress scale after exercise than before exercise.
- Focus, concentration, and memory improve. Blood

flow to the brain is increased during a workout of any kind, and this increase can last for most of your day, even if the exercise was fairly brief.
- Your mood becomes more stable. Your ability to regulate your emotions increases, which causes your feelings to be less erratic. Even the frequency, duration, and severity of extreme mood alterations like depressive or manic episodes are decreased.
- You sleep and eat better and have more energy overall. Your brain increases the production of norepinephrine, a neurotransmitter that helps to regulate physical functioning and activation.
- Increased cognitive "flexibility." Neuroplasticity is bolstered, which helps you be less rigid in your thinking and behavior and more open to new experiences or ideas.
- Better decision-making. Various brain structures relating to executive functioning are turbocharged by exercise-related endorphin releases, which help you see things more clearly.

Essentially, exercise makes you into a neurological superbeing. It keeps you at the top of your game, forces your brain to be the best version of itself that it's capable of being. It accomplishes just about everything we try to achieve with caffeine (energy and focus), alcohol (lower stress), supplements (better sleep and appetite), and psychiatric medications (more emotional stability and mental flexibility), and it does it with virtually no consequences. It is a secret weapon in this war.

If your vision of regular physical activity involves a sweat-drenched face, struggling to catch a breath, and collapsing onto the floor in exhaustion after it's over, banish those thoughts right now. Regular, moderate-intensity physical activity is the goal. Pushing your workout beyond a moderate level of intensity doesn't appear to have any additional mental health benefits that we've been able to show consistently. The most common outcome of a high-intensity workout is not wanting to work out the following day.

The intensity of a workout is determined in part by your current physical fitness level. In other words, if you're a relatively sedentary person, you won't have to work very hard to reach a moderate-intensity level of exercise. A brisk walk might do the trick.

It doesn't have to be a massive test of endurance either. Reports of ideal frequency and duration vary from study to study, but they generally range from 20 to 40 minutes a day, 3 to 5 days a week. You don't need to execute 2-hour daily workouts to start feeling better. Try to create a sustainable routine. If you make a workout plan that you dread, you're eventually going to stop doing it.

Assuming it meets the above guidelines for frequency, intensity, and duration, the type of physical activity makes no difference whatsoever. Just pick something you find at least moderately enjoyable, or if that's an unrealistic goal, do whatever you find the least unpleasant. Remember that this is a habit we want to continue for the rest of your life, and people don't tend to stick to things that they despise doing. Disregard any biases you hold about what types of activity are "better" or "worse." They're all equally beneficial for your mental health.

As you work on establishing your fitness routine, I want you to start small. The numbers I quoted above, 20 to 40 minutes a day, 3 to 5 days a week, are the long-term goals. Start on the low end of that range or even below it. We want to make these changes gradually to help them be sustainable. Ask yourself, "what can I start with today?" and just commit to that for now. If that's taking a 5-minute walk three days a week, do that. When that starts to feel too easy, that's when you should think about increasing the frequency or the duration.

Remember This:

Try to establish a physical activity routine that's appropriate for your current fitness level. Don't do this for aesthetic purposes like fat loss or muscle building, but for cognitive and emotional health. Start slow, and work your way up to your desired routine gradually to prevent burnout.

SHUT IT DOWN

Are you tired (see what I did there?) of fighting a battle to fall asleep? It's beyond frustrating to try and coax your mind into shutting off when you know you need a few good hours of sleep to have any hope of having a decent day tomorrow. I wish we had been designed with a "deactivate" switch, and we could just shut ourselves down when we needed to rest. Getting yourself to fall asleep is a frustratingly delicate process that requires much more finesse than willpower. Try as you might, you can't force your mind to turn off by reminding yourself of how desperately you need sleep and how awful tomorrow will be if you're exhausted. If you don't want sleep to be a battle, you'll need to understand your brain waves.

Beta brain waves occur during awake, alert states. Your brain is probably producing mostly beta waves right now as you're reading this passage. Any task that requires conscious focus and attention facilitates beta wave production. Activities like school, work, social engagement, taking care of your house, and most of your hobbies run primarily on beta brain waves.

Alpha brain waves occur during awake but relaxed and restful states. You're still conscious and thinking, but it's a state of alertness that people often describe as "slower" and "deeper." The moments just before you fall asleep and shortly after you awaken are alpha brain wave moments. So are the periods during and after calming, relaxing activities like massage and meditation. Many people experience a rush of alpha wave production after a workout, sex, or other types of physical exertion. Alpha brain wave production at or around whatever time of day you typically fall asleep is what helps your mind "shut down" and enables you to rest.

Theta brain waves occur during periods of semi-consciousness. Lighter sleep stages involving dreaming, dissociative episodes, or deep meditative states, to provide a few examples. Even if you're asleep during theta wave production, you maintain some awareness of and responsiveness to your environment. The classic "falling dream that wakes you up" is an excellent example of this. You're somewhere on the bridge between consciousness and unconsciousness.

Delta brain waves occur during periods of deep, restful sleep. This is the closest your brain ever gets to "shutting off" while you're still among the living. It's minimal activity mode, the most restful and restorative state of being.

Shifting brain wave states takes a little bit of time. Your mind needs a period of time to adjust functioning to new activities, so you can't just instantly switch from one mode to the next. Falling asleep occurs somewhere in the transition from alpha to theta. You can't fall asleep when your brain is in beta wave mode unless you literally pass out from exhaustion. They're incompatible psychological states.

Spending time on tasks or activities that facilitate beta brain wave production right up until the moment you get into bed and try to fall asleep is guaranteed to make falling asleep feel like a battle. You need to allow your brain time to shift gradually into alpha and theta wave production mode. I know you're an incredibly busy person with a seemingly unlimited amount of tasks that need doing, but you aren't doing yourself any favors trying to cram one or two more achievements in just before bed.

Late at night might seem like an ideal time to squeeze in a little extra uninterrupted work, but you'll pay for it exponentially the following day. Getting even one or two fewer hours of sleep than your ideal amount decreases processing speed and overall productivity by around 20% on average the next day. In a 16-hour day, a 20% decrease in productivity costs you just over 3 hours worth of output. Put another way, if you stay up 2 hours late to get some work done, you lose an hour of net productivity the following day. It's not worth it. Don't do it.

Instead, designate the time before you go to bed as a little window reserved exclusively for calm, relaxing activities to facilitate alpha wave production and help you fall asleep more quickly once your head hits your pillow. Aromatherapy using calming scents like lavender, whether from body lotion, candles, essential oils, shower gel, or any other source helps get your brain in a sleeping mindset. Light progressive muscle relaxation, even very low-intensity yoga, can help reduce physical tension, which puts your mind at ease. Doing a few minutes of deep breathing or meditation can stimulate alpha wave production, as we also breathe more slowly and deeply while we sleep.

Being consistent with your before-bed activities also helps with sleep initiation. You can condition your mind to associate certain stimuli or actions with a restful state if you consistently do them before going to bed. Try to establish and maintain a consistent before-bed routine like showering, putting on pajamas, washing your face, and brushing your teeth at around the same time every night to provide your brain with cues that you want to fall asleep soon.

You should also consider the qualities of your sleep environment. Creating and maintaining a physical environment conducive to entering a restful state will speed up the sleep initiation process. Light of any kind, natural or artificial, has a stimulating effect on the mind. Bright lights signal to our nervous system that something important is taking place, which encourages the production of beta waves and motivates our brains to stay awake and alert. Try to make your sleeping environment as dark as you're willing to tolerate. Consider room darkening shades if possible.

Sound can be just as important as light when it comes to sleep. Your auditory system stays online even when you're in the deepest stages of sleep, which is why you can be startled awake by loud sounds in the middle of the night. This is another survival mechanism, as loud sounds at night were a telltale sign of imminent danger when we were a more primal, nomadic people. There's nothing wrong with needing some noise to fall asleep, but try to use static sounds like box fans, white noise machines, or nature sounds instead of dynamic sounds like shows or music.

If the last couple hours of your day are generally your favorite, I understand. The day is full of stressors, tasks, people, and stimulation. Even if it's all good things, it still takes a lot out of you. There's nothing quite like the quiet, still calm of the night, and I want you to be able to enjoy that. I don't want you to enjoy it so much that you suffer the following day because of it. There is nothing more beneficial that you can do during your designated sleeping time for both your physical and mental health than being asleep.

Getting an adequate amount of sleep will almost certainly reduce your stress level the following day so much more than watching one more episode of your show or reading one more chapter in your book. Our brains work differently when we get enough sleep. We are calmer, more composed, and more resilient. Sleep is always worth it.

Lastly, be mindful of your use of substances around the time you go to sleep. Caffeine can cause acute mild insomnia if ingested within 8 hours of bedtime. Even if it doesn't impair your ability to fall asleep, it negatively impacts your progression through the cycles of sleep and, in turn, your mood and your productivity the following day. Even relaxing or sedating substances like alcohol, marijuana, and antihistamines impair your ability to reach the deeper stages of sleep. It's better to get 6 hours of natural sleep than 8 hours of sleep assisted by these drugs.

Please take sleep seriously. Its importance cannot be overstated. It is an absolutely fundamental building block of physical health, mental health, and longevity. I'm genuinely not convinced it's possible to achieve a reasonable state of mental health without having at least decent sleeping habits.

Remember This:

Make sleep a priority in your life. Getting enough will enhance almost every aspect of your life and your functioning, including your emotional health. Designate the period of time before going to bed as a "work-free" zone and reserve that 30-to-60-minute window for calm, relaxing activities. Try to avoid substances like alcohol or caffeine within a few hours of bedtime to improve your sleep quality.

DARK

Why is it so dark all the time?
Even during the day it's dark.
The sky is dark.
The water is dark.
The buildings are dark.
I like rainy days the best, because at least then everyone sees it.
They make me feel at home, cozy, comforted.
They're the only time that the world looks how I feel.
I wish it could always be raining.
And overcast.
And just a little chilly.
I try to sleep all day because the sun just doesn't feel right.
I like when there's just a little bit of light.
A street lamp or a headlight.
But otherwise black.
That's how it feels inside.
That's how I like it.

FUEL

Many of your electronic devices have some sort of power-saving mode. When the battery is nearly depleted, the device limits itself to essential functions to preserve what little energy remains in the charge. The goal is to stave off a total shut down for as long as possible, even if that means the device demonstrates frustratingly impaired functioning in the meantime. The screen becomes so dim it can be hard to read. Applications load and run slowly. Some won't run at all.

You also have a power-saving mode. When your brain lacks critical resources needed for optimal functioning, it also limits itself to essential functions to preserve what little energy remains inside of you. The result is a predictable set of behavioral and psychological changes. Human power-saving mode looks like this:

Irritability

Difficulty paying attention

Nervousness

Problems falling or staying asleep

Confusion

Fatigue

Dizziness

Shakiness

Lethargy

Racing heart

Headache

Nausea

Mood swings

From a mental health perspective, this could be describing several possible conditions. Irritability, nervousness, racing heart, difficulty concentrating, and headaches are all symptoms of anxiety. Throw in dizziness, shakiness, nausea, and confusion, and this may be a full-blown panic attack. Difficulty concentrating, lethargy, and mood swings are symptoms of mood disorders like major depressive disorder or bipolar disorder. The condition that best captures all of these comorbid symptoms isn't a psychiatric issue at all; it's hunger.

Keeping your mind and body appropriately nourished is just as important for your cognitive and emotional health as getting adequate sleep. Your metabolic rate, the process that largely influences hunger and digestion, rises and falls in waves like the stages of sleep. As with your circadian rhythm, you can somewhat customize the rise and fall of these waves to match your daily routine (assuming you have one.) And when these habits have been "off" for a long time, it becomes very, very difficult to make any meaningful progress in managing your mental health without re-establishing them.

Timing is crucial. Your body can process food so much more efficiently if you generally eat at around the same times each day. Creating this consistency causes your metabolic rate to increase during what your body anticipates will be a mealtime. You'll feel hunger more naturally and digest food more easily at these times. When you regularly skip a specific meal, you train your body to slow down its metabolic rate during that period of your day. This diminishes your hunger cues and causes your body to disregard its physiological needs. Put another way, your feelings of hunger (or lack thereof) have much more to do with the habits you are in than whether you need food at any given time.

Food, dieting, and overall health management have all become industries. As with any industry, the main focus is the bottom line of the corporation, not the health of the customer. Food manufacturers, generally speaking, do not care about you. They will trick you. They will lie to you. They will use you as a test subject for their products.

Most commercially available food products today are the outcome of millions of dollars and thousands of hours worth of laboratory research. The purpose of all of this research is to create a product that is as addictive as possible and as cheap as possible to maximize company profits. Food engineers seek to replicate the "addiction zone" where food is as delicious as possible but minimally satisfying, encouraging you to over-consume it and therefore buy more of it.

The excess saturation of cooking oils and artificial sweeteners in modern commercial foods creates blood sugar peaks and valleys that have you chasing your next "high." Consuming sugary, fatty snack foods gives you a brief boost in energy and mood. Within two to three hours, you start to "crash" and subconsciously begin seeking out more high-sugar snacks to chase that high and feel OK again.

If you want your relationship with food to support your mental health, you're going to have to pay close attention to the foods you purchase. You can't just eat highly processed snack foods all day and expect to feel OK. We aren't designed for that. If you don't want to experience a physiologically driven state of emotional turmoil every day, you're going to have to step off the blood sugar rollercoaster and return to your nutritional roots (Get it? Roots?)

I'm the wrong type of doctor to explain why eating minimally processed foods is better for your physical health, but I know that doing so is vital to manage your mental health. Foods with fewer sweeteners, cooking oils, and other additives don't create the crazy blood sugar highs and lows that wreak havoc on your focus, concentration, and emotional regulation. It's not a coincidence that the commercial that coined the term "hangry" was for a Snickers bar.

You don't have to go crazy about this. As with any behavioral change, it's best to start small and be gradual if you want to create new habits that will stick. Maybe you swap out your evening chips for some carrots. Perhaps you bring nuts or trail mix to work instead of donuts. Start with one thing. Stay with that one thing until it feels normal. Don't rush yourself. We like to create artificial stress around food and eating, but you have your entire life to figure this out, and nobody ever masters it because the science that informs it is constantly evolving.

Maintaining emotional stability throughout your day will also be easier if you don't skip meals. I'm not talking about fasting, where not eating during a certain period of the day is intentional and consistent and overall caloric intake remains adequate. I'm talking about the days when you wake up late and decide to skip breakfast, or the busy days where you work through lunch, or the poor body image days where you try not to eat dinner. Your body and mind are counting on receiving nourishment during these times. When you refuse to provide them with the regular nutrition and resources they expect, you're likely to trigger human low power mode. Your mind needs caloric energy from food just as badly as it needs oxygen from the air.

Remember that your brain does its best work when you're as consistent as possible in managing your biology. Because of this, I am very anti-diet. Diets encourage making dramatic changes to your eating habits, and then at some point changing them back again (because most diets are only meant to be followed for a short time to avoid nutritional deficiencies). Temporary changes in your routine will produce only temporary changes elsewhere. Following a highly restrictive diet for three months and then returning to regular eating habits and thinking this will somehow make you healthier is like putting 50% of your income into your 401k for three months and then thinking you could retire. As with so many things in life, consistency is the key when it comes to eating.

Please care for your body with the love, respect, and dignity it deserves. You'll probably never get another one, although my love of all things science fiction makes me hesitant to guarantee this.

Remember This:

Food and mental health are intrinsically linked. Your brain does not function correctly without a regular supply of high-quality caloric energy. Make sure to give it the resources it needs to do its best work.

RECHARGE

Energy is confusing. Sometimes you'll have a day full of tasks with constant activity and minimal breaks, yet by the end of it all you don't feel half as exhausted as you expected to. On other days you do almost nothing, yet you're ready for a nap by early afternoon.

Being busy isn't inherently draining. If it's all day every day that will absolutely catch up to you, but productivity and accomplishments can be energizing if you value what you're doing and have a reasonable degree of confidence in your abilities. It's stress, not busyness, that's the culprit of most fatigue. And you can be stressed out without doing anything at all. In fact, sometimes doing nothing at all is our biggest stressor.

It takes just as much mental energy to think about doing something as it does to do that thing. To your brain, there's no major distinction between planning, worrying, visualizing, and anticipating behaviors and physically executing these behaviors. The only difference is whether your brain sends a signal to your nervous system to complete the behavior or not. Conceptualization is just as taxing on your mental energy reserves as execution.

Mental energy is a finite property. You only have so much of it each day. You can get little boosts here and there through effective use of breaks, but when it's gone, that's the end of your productivity for that day. We've all felt it. You still have things you want to get done, but no matter how much guilt yourself, shame yourself, or promise yourself rewards, your body just won't get off the couch and your brain feels like a blank chalkboard. You've reached your limit for that day.

When we feel worn down or exhausted, we often crave downtime. This doesn't always produce the expected results. Downtime is restful for the body, but it can be stressful for the mind. The less engaged and occupied your brain is by whatever is happening around you, the more freedom it has to wander. For most of us, our minds like to wander towards distress, regret, and other stressful internal stimuli. Your mind may be working harder during this supposed "downtime" than during the busier parts of your day. What you really need in those moments is a recharge.

There are three properties of an effective recharging activity; high stimulation, low stress, and novel. A high stimulation activity is an activity that takes most of your conscious attention to engage in and that you feel naturally drawn towards. Something that uses your entire brain and doesn't give it any freedom to wander its way back to whatever happens to be bothering you. Something that locks you in and makes time fly.

Low stress seems self-explanatory, but I've observed that some people are terrible at differentiating between what they do and don't find stressful. Watching sports comes to mind; it *seems* like a low-stress activity, yet the amount of yelling, screaming, and general exacerbation that often accompanies it suggests otherwise.

I define a low-stress activity as any activity in which you are not terribly invested in the outcome. No matter how things turn out, it isn't going to ruin your day. For example, I find woodworking low-stress because I'm bad at it and I know I'm bad at it, and I don't expect to produce anything that doesn't become firewood. I'm totally fine with that outcome. If I were trying to sell my sad little carvings on Etsy, woodworking wouldn't be low-stress.

To keep things novel, you have to switch things up every now and then. If you go back to the same few things over and over again, your brain eventually becomes a little too good at those things and they stop requiring conscious effort. Once your mind starts "filling in the blanks" for you, that activity doesn't require as much conscious attention from you, and it starts to lose its ability to distract you from your stress.

You don't necessarily need to change hobbies dramatically or develop brand new interests. Just keep things fresh. Try to find a new musical artist or even a new genre. If you normally watch action movies, try a documentary. If you mostly read self-help books (low blow?), grab a sci-fi novel. If you love running, try a team sport. Keep your mind occupied with newness so that it isn't allowed to ruminate endlessly on the same doom scenarios.

Remember This:

It isn't action that drains you; it's stress. Taking breaks or extended time off from work or other stressors won't always recharge you; sometimes it makes you feel worse. To effectively recharge yourself, seek out activities that are high stimulation but low stress, and switch them up regularly so that they stay novel and engaging to your mind.

DARK PART 2

You're going to hate me for saying this.
I would too.
But it isn't actually dark all the time.
That's just your perception.
You're going to come back here one day.
You're going to expect it to look the same.
Gray, brown, and lifeless.
But it won't.
There will be blues, greens, reds.
You'll wonder when the city changed.
It didn't.
That's what it's always looked like.
You just don't see it right now.
And that's OK.
It isn't your fault.
It isn't something you're doing wrong.
It's just where you're at right now.
Someday rainy days won't feel like home anymore.
They'll just feel wet.

SHAME EXECUTIONER

Shame is a saboteur. It loves secrecy, thrives upon it. Shame lurks in the shadows of pain, rejection, and failure. It does its best work in the dark, where it can move unseen. It waits patiently and silently, ever-vigilant of your experience of feelings that contradict it. Pride. Excitement. Connection. Validation. When these feelings arise, shame makes it move. It darts from the dark recesses of your mind and pounces on the positive feelings. It presses a blade to their throat, and they're gone as quickly as they came. Shame recedes to the darkness, waiting for its next moment.

We are born shameless. The seeds of shame are planted in our minds by others who tell us or show us that, in their eyes, we aren't good enough, smart enough, or attractive enough. We water these seeds by aligning with the messages that planted them and living our lives in accordance with them. If we were shamed for our abilities, we avoid using those abilities. If we were shamed for our looks, we hide our appearance.

When we hide what we've been told are the unacceptable, unglamorous, and unlovable parts of ourselves, we provide shame with the environment it needs in order to thrive; darkness. The more pieces of ourselves we hide from others, the more internal space we allocate for the shame within. It takes root inside of us, becoming inseparable from our core being. It's an emotional cancer that grows over time, reinforced and strengthened every time we judge, criticize, and insult ourselves.

There's a way that you can execute the shame. Destroy its

native environment. The fewer parts of yourself that you hide from others, the fewer places shame can hide within you. Once it has nowhere left to go, you can drag it out into the light and expose it. Shame can't handle exposure. That's why it constantly encourages you to hide, to avoid, and to retreat; that's the only way it can continue to grow inside of you.

By sharing something painful that has happened to you, something you're not proud of, or something others have shamed you for, you challenge the message that allowed the shame to take root. You reject the theory that you need to keep this experience hidden from others. You reinforce to yourself that you continue to deserve love, appreciation, and respect despite your imperfections.

If the other person validates or empathizes with you, that light becomes even brighter still and might melt the shame away entirely. But that part isn't essential to executing your shame; it's just a bonus. What kills the shame is your refusal to hide yourself any longer. Hiding truths about yourself is the genesis of the shame within. Nobody can effectively shame you for that which you are unashamed of. They may still try, but it will bounce right off. Your refusal to validate their insults immunizes you.

Disclosure about who you are and what you've been through does need to be strategic. Not everyone deserves to know everything about you. Some may use the personal information you share against you or for their own gain. But chronic, habitual secrecy creates a deep and pervasive well of shame within ourselves. The hidden message that we are reinforcing to ourselves every time we try to control what other people see is "the truth about who you are and what you've done is awful."

What could show more strength, more courage, and more bravery than metaphorically dropping your armor? Lies, deceptions, and manipulations may earn you favorable appraisals from others, but they eat away at you internally. Each corrodes your sense of worthiness and value, leaving in the void a single, damning phrase; "I am not good enough."

Remember This:

Shame grows when we shelter it and withers when we're open about it. Try not to hide the parts of yourself that you dislike quite so much, at least not from everyone.

PART IV: THE BEGINNING

"If anything from this book starts to fade, just come back. You have me forever now."

REMEMBER ME

If you've made it this far, I assume you found something you were looking for. Let's make sure you keep it. Whatever you're feeling right now, it won't last forever. You might forget some of what we've talked about, even parts that seemed to mean everything to you when you first read them. It's just how our minds work.

If anything from this book starts to fade, just come back. You have me forever now. If it were up to me, here's what I would want you to remember from our time together:

Your body, your mind, your soul, and your life itself belong to you. Changing them exclusively for the sake of other people isn't noble. It's one of the most dangerous and destructive things you can do. It robs the world of a unique presence and leaves in its place a statistical average. It creates a void upon this earth where you should be standing.

Ask questions constantly. Gather as much data about yourself as possible and never let assumptions dictate the course of your life. Your mind tries to automate as many processes as possible, which in theory is a wonderful thing, but sometimes it automates glitches and coding errors. These errors will run again and again and hold you back from living your best life unless you find them and fix them.
Questions help you find them.

Look for the patterns that kill your feelings. Your emotions aren't the enemy – the patterns are. We learn to numb, to hide, and to invalidate. Living this way drains our passion, steals our excitement. Life becomes an emotional flatline. Stopping the patterns reclaims your feelings.

Try to avoid the pull of the familiar, the gravity of other people. The default human condition is to remain the same and avoid change, especially if those around you are somewhat stagnant in their own lives. There's an instinctual desire to live like them and align with them. You'll have to fight against that if you want more from your life than what they have.

Consider rejecting the unrealistic and inappropriate blame you're expected to place upon yourself. There are so many messages out there encouraging us to take full control and responsibility for our lives which completely ignore the reality of the human experience. We don't get to choose our circumstances or our situations for the most formative years of our lives, and some of those experiences permanently change us.

You don't have to change the world to be powerful. Changing what happens inside yourself will make more of a difference in your life than anything you could do to change the outer world. You may not be in a position of social power, but you'll always have more control over yourself than anyone else will.

The hollow, empty, incomplete feeling you get sometimes is the hole where your relationship with yourself should be. Trying to fill it with other things is a dead end; that relationship is irreplaceable. Other people, things, and achievements can never be an adequate substitution. If you don't devote time and energy to yourself, nothing else you have will matter.

Whatever feels "right" to you is what you've heard most frequently. That doesn't mean it's real. Repetition of information causes our brains to regard that information as factual, even if it's fictional or subjective. That's how you can come to believe terrible things about yourself, "truths" that are contradicted every day. Practicing repetition of new truths can override false, unhelpful messages.

Trying too hard produces the same results as not trying hard enough. Most people live under an utterly dysfunctional amount of pressure and stress. When we're less productive than we think we should be, we usually respond by adding more pressure and stress, which further buries us. Patience, understanding, and stress management are so much more important for meeting your goals than willpower, motivation, or accountability.

You're more ready than you feel. Your emotions aren't always a great predictor of your abilities. Our brains haven't evolved nearly as quickly as our society and our lifestyles, and some of your responses are outdated and obsolete. You can teach your brain that you're farther along than it recognizes by taking action before you feel completely prepared to do so.

The critical voice in your head isn't yours. Those thoughts and statements were mostly placed there by other people. When you start repeating the judgments, criticisms, and abuse you've heard from others in your own voice, you claim them as your own and they become harder to ignore. Mentally giving these thoughts to someone else helps you challenge them.

Almost everything you consider to be knowledge is just a theory. Very few things in this life can truly be known. Once we think we know something, we stop looking for evidence to the contrary and put on blinders that we can wear for our entire lives. Reconceptualizing what you think you know as a theory and testing your theories frequently can unlock so many doors.

You can protect yourself from the thoughts, feelings, and beliefs of other people by creating and guarding your own private mental space. Sometimes the lines between ourselves and other people become blurred. It's easy to automatically absorb their beliefs and values if you don't consciously guard your mind against unwanted influence.

The only person who sees most of what you do is you. The majority of the best and most important things you do in a day are internal and invisible to most people. You are the only one who can acknowledge and reinforce your inner victories, but most of us don't celebrate ourselves very often. Consciously taking notice of all the things you do right in a day can dramatically change your perspective of yourself.

Being productive and accomplishing your goals isn't a matter of motivation or willpower; it's simple math. An instinctual comparison of effort and reward. Using mental strategies to make behaviors require less effort or produce stronger feelings of reward can override your natural resistance to task completion and help you develop healthier habits and a more productive lifestyle.

Your mind has a glitch that happens when it tries to predict the future. It doesn't know how to extrapolate for personal growth and change, so it uses your present self as a surrogate to predict the outcomes of your future plans. This causes you to hold yourself back from opportunity and challenge because you have a hard time committing to doing anything in the future that you don't currently feel capable of doing. If you start to trust that you'll evolve along the way to your destination, you can stop living a step or two behind your true potential.

Asking the wrong questions can freeze you. It's so easy to become obsessed with big, philosophical, generally unanswerable questions. Life is much too complicated for us to ever really understand why things happen or what could have been. Focus more on your present needs than your past regrets, and start asking questions that have useful, actionable answers.

When the past bleeds into the present, life can become an infinite loop. Anticipating and trying to avoid the suffering we've experienced in the past can paradoxically cause the same pain to reoccur over and over again. Being hypervigilant in relationships often turns into a self-fulfilling prophecy. If you can release people from your patterns, you'll probably get hurt a lot less often.

The only person you truly know is you. Your knowledge of other people, even those close to you, is mostly surface level. Try to resist the temptation to constantly compare yourself to others; you aren't comparing alike things. You don't really know what's going on inside of anybody except you. The only metric that matters is whether you feel like you're on a path that will lead you to your personal goals.

Your past wasn't simpler; you were simpler in your past. That's why every generation of humanity looks back fondly on the "good old days" but never feels that way about the present; they have an unrealistically positive recall of their childhoods because their young minds were ignorant to the stressors and problems going on around them. Trying to chase the past is a mistake; there are moments in your present that are just as good, and they'll pass you by every day if you aren't looking out for them.

Having a good life won't automatically fill you with feelings of gratitude. Being grateful for whatever you have is a skill that requires strategy and practice. Being too vague and broad with your attempts at gratitude or using the wonderful parts of your life to shame or invalidate yourself won't produce a genuine appreciation for your life. To experience genuine gratitude, you have to be as specific as possible and avoid the comparison trap.

Most people have one or two feelings that feel better to them than other pleasant feelings. Knowing what your favorite emotions are can provide tremendous guidance in life and help you reduce the absolutely overwhelming amount of choices available to you. Knowing what you really want out of this life and turning that insight into a simple question you ask yourself regularly will narrow down the big choices you have to make.

You can't force self-love through self-improvement. The way you feel about yourself is determined so much more by how much or how little of your time, energy, and attention you invest in yourself than by meeting arbitrary goals. Setting benchmarks for yourself and withholding love from yourself until you meet them isn't growth; it's internal emotional abuse. Invest in yourself now to generate the feelings that propel you forward.

Our pain often hides our gifts. Sometimes people make being different in any way extremely unpleasant for us. We often learn to hide the most unique, important, remarkable parts of ourselves because of the unwanted attention they bring. Without a strong sense of purpose and meaning in your life, you're vulnerable to nihilism and emptiness. Try to reclaim what you've buried and allow the parts of yourself that are "different" to come to the forefront again.

The most direct route to confidence is discomfort. Seek out the middle ground between your comfort zone and things that currently overwhelm you and try to spend some time in that middle ground every day. Eventually those things become a part of your comfort zone and you're able to move on to the next most challenging thing. Over time, this can completely change your experience of living in this world and give you confidence and trust in yourself beyond what you might think is possible.

Your brain isn't the same every day. It has good days and bad days, and regular physical activity helps keep it at the top of its range. Keeping that blood and oxygen flowing enables you to be the best possible version of yourself. Be consistent, keep the duration relatively brief and the intensity moderate, and do what you enjoy the most rather than what you've been told is the best.

There's no substitute for sleep. Nothing can replace the absolutely vital role rest plays in your mental health. If you do everything right but you aren't getting enough sleep you'll still feel awful. It is unavoidably essential, and treating it as an inconvenience tends to lead to insomnia, poor sleep quality, and an unsatisfactory life.

Your brain needs regular access to food just as much as it needs regular access to oxygen. Eating more foods that aren't overly modified or manufactured can have a stabilizing effect on your mood. Try not to skip meals or go too long without eating to avoid blood sugar related mood crashes.

Being busy doesn't exhaust you nearly as much as stress exhausts you. You can be busy without being stressed, and you can be stressed without being busy. Maintaining your energy and motivation isn't about avoiding hard work; it's about keeping your mind occupied with high-stimulation, low-stress, novel activities.

You can kill shame. It can only thrive within you if you create and maintain a welcoming environment for it. Hiding parts of yourself, blaming yourself for your suffering, and refusing to honor what makes you different or unique creates a perfect ecosystem for shame to grow in. It expands from within, creeping across your mind to claim new territory and making less space for emotions like pride, joy, excitement, or accomplishment. Refusing to run or hide and owning who you are destroys its native environment. It cannot thrive within you if you don't create a space for it.

That's it. Those are the most important skills and concepts I've learned in 37 years of being alive and 12 years of providing therapy. They're the reason I'm still alive. They're the reason I can help people when others often can't. I've built a life beyond what I would have ever thought possible for someone like me, and now you know how I did it. If any of my experiences, my feelings, or my memoirs landed for you, it probably means there's enough common ground between us that at least some of what worked for me will also work for you. Try them out.

Take what you like and leave what you don't care for. Tweak and modify my ideas to make them work better for you. Claim this work and make it your own. That's ultimately what I did to get here.

THE BEGINNING

This can be the beginning if you want it to. The new start of your journey you first set off on so long ago. The past is so powerful. Patterns are so persistent. You'll feel pulled to go back again. Your mind will start to doubt the legitimacy of everything we've talked about. The old pathways will call to you again. It'll be hard to resist going back.

Resist.

Refuse.

Deny.

Defy.

It can help you break away from them if you make some type of clear mental delineation between past and present, then and now.

It's this.

Right now.

You will never feel these exact sensations again, will never read these words for the first time beyond this precise moment. Every moment before this one is now "then." That was still you, but that was old you. New you starts right now. New you knows things that old you didn't understand. New you has tools that old you never had access to. New you is something entirely different, something you've never seen before.

It's possible to reach a point where you don't have to run

from the dark thoughts of your mind anymore. Claim enough victories over them, and they'll start to run from you. They can't stand up to any real questions or assessments. They bully you into listening with volume, aggression, and fear because there's nothing of substance behind their words. Once you know how to see that, they're done for. You'll become a warrior descending into their midst, protected by your bubble, armed with the truth. They will scatter when you arrive.

You're not alone. So many people are fighting their own version of your battle every day. Some of them are reading this very book right now. Your goals, your dreams, and your buried feelings are knocking on the door. They're stranded out in the rain, drenched, shivering, waiting to come in.

Will you let them in?

Don't you dare give yourself a time limit.

Don't lose sight of the immensity of what you're doing. Here's the tale of the tape.

You're up against:

- Your genetics
- The habits of your ancestors
- Evolution, or lack thereof
- Society at large

On your side, we have:

- A book
- Maybe a few very supportive people
- Maybe a therapist (and if you don't have one, I strongly recommend trying to find one. A good therapist is invaluable and irreplaceable.)
- Yourself

Those odds may look bleak to you, but I like them, mostly because of that final bullet point. You are the trump card in this game, the secret weapon in this war, the deus ex machine in this story.

You're a ninja who can work unseen. You can self-regulate, set boundaries, and change thought patterns without anyone noticing. Nothing can stop the work you do in the shadows of your own mind.

You're supersonic. You can know what's going on inside of you and react to it before anyone or anything else knows what's happened. If you listen to yourself and pay attention to your internal experience, you can solve so many problems before they even exist outside of you.

You're omnipresent. So much of your experience in this life is exclusively internal. You know what nobody else knows and see what's invisible to them. And you can act on the knowledge that only you have access to.

You've got you forever. And now you have parts of me forever too. Take your favorite phrases from this book, the concepts you found most useful, and practice them until they become a natural part of your thought process. Program them into yourself the way all those unhelpful messages were programmed into you so long ago; through sustained repetition. Load helpful messages into your subconscious, where they can be antibodies to the brokenness and the pain you've absorbed. Take anything you want from our time together. It's all here for you.

Yes, I like our odds. I like our odds quite a lot.

HAUNTED

It still isn't gone.

I'm beginning to accept that it may never be gone.

I can still sense it. Stalking me. Following me.

But it's farther behind me than it's ever been.

And for the first time in my life, I think I'm gaining ground.

This might be the closest to victory that I'll ever know.

I gladly accept it.

It's more than I ever expected.

More than I ever dreamed.

I didn't even think I'd live this long.

Didn't imagine I could ever help anyone.

Never thought I would cry tears of joy.

Yet somehow, I've done all of these things.

In spite of being a haunted human.

Or maybe, in a strange way, because of it.

I think I've finally found a purpose for it all.

Living through it is the only reason I'm able to speak to you in this manner.

The things that follow me are the only reasons I was able to write this book.

I wonder what you will do with yours.

Please show me.

Please tell me.

I'll be waiting.

To hear all about it.

SOUNDTRACK

I could never have written these words without my playlist. It evolved over the course of this work, but there were a few artists who were a constant from beginning to end. I want to give special mention to them here.

Vindu

Swarm

Moris Black

Raimu

Huey Daze

Elijah Nang

City Girl

Cable

Sierra

Tenno

Danisogen

Infraction

Matteo Tura

THANK YOU!!

It means the world to me that you chose to read this work from start to finish (assuming you didn't just skip to this page for some odd reason. If you did, get out of here! I'll see you soon.) I'm a fully independent author with no editor (hopefully that wasn't painfully obvious!), focus group, or marketing team. Every word you've read was chosen and arranged by me. Some came from my mind, some came from my heart, and some came from a part of me that doesn't have a name. People like you are the only reason this book exists and the only reason anyone else knows about this book.

I didn't know what obsession was before writing this. It started as a hobby, but once it neared completion, it took over my life. I couldn't go a day without writing, couldn't sleep until I got my thoughts out each night. I put absolutely everything I had into this, and I hope something within was helpful to you.

If you enjoyed this work, it would help me tremendously if you would leave a review on Amazon! I love hearing about people's authentic reactions to my work, and it also helps other people find this book. You can also find me on Instagram at @dr.scott.eilers. I hope to hear from you soon!

- Scott

Printed in Great Britain
by Amazon

36710972R00136